WRIGHT SITES

A Guide to
Frank Lloyd Wright
Public Places

Edited by
Arlene Sanderson

Introduction by
Jack Quinan

Revised
Second Edition

PRINCETON ARCHITECTURAL PRESS

Published by
Princeton Architectural Press
37 East 7th Street
New York, New York 10003
(212) 995-9620

Cover design by Don Bergh, Chicago
Book design and production by Allison Saltzman
Printed and bound in the United States

Library of Congress Cataloging-in-Publication Data
Wright Sites : a guide to Frank Lloyd Wright public places / edited by Arlene Sanderson ;
introduction by Jack Quinan. – – 2nd ed., rev.
p. cm.
Includes bibliographical references and index.
ISBN 1-56898-041-8 (alk. paper)
1. Wright, Frank Lloyd, 1867–1959 – – Themes, motives.
2. Architecture, Modern – – 20th century – – United States – – Guidebooks.
I. Sanderson, Arlene, 1953–   .
NA737.W7W75   1995
720'.92– –dc20   95-24042   CIP

On the cover: entrance to the Susan Lawrence Dana House, Springfield, Illinois
Photograph by Doug Carr, courtesy of the Dana-Thomas House State Historic Site

For a free catalog of other books published by Princeton Architectural Press, call toll free (800) 458-1131

CONTENTS

FOREWORD

The plays of William Shakespeare, the artwork of Pablo Picasso, the designs of Frank Lloyd Wright. These are some of the greatest artistic achievements of our culture, and are appreciated by millions worldwide.

Shakespeare's works are performed daily around the globe; videotapes of his plays are available widely; his sonnets and the scripts to his plays can be purchased for a few dollars from any bookstore. Many of Picasso's greatest paintings and sculptures reside in museums available for anyone to enjoy. The rest of his work is in private hands, but respectfully cared for. We can be certain that our children and those in the distant future will be able to enjoy Shakespeare's and Picasso's work—their long-term survival is unquestioned.

But, the future of most of Frank Lloyd Wright's work is not assured.

One in five of his buildings has been demolished. Others have suffered in the past from neglect or unsympathetic owners who have altered them insensitively. A few owners continue to strip their houses, selling off art-glass windows and furniture that Wright designed specifically for the building.

Fortunately, today, most Wright building owners are conscientious stewards, but they must nonetheless struggle with their buildings' ongoing deterioration. Wright delighted in trying out experimental construction technologies, and loading structural members to their maximum. As a consequence, all owners face unusual problems when their buildings require the inevitable specialized construction or preservation assistance that often involves materials the average contractor or architect has never even seen. Beyond the drain of maintenance and restoration, the financial, legal, and ethical complexities of ownership can overwhelm the most enlightened and resourceful of individuals.

The noted architecture critic Robert Campbell has warned, "No issue of architectural preservation in the United States is more important or more urgent than that of the

Wright houses." Former dean of architecture at Yale University Thomas Beeby has written, "Without an overall plan to save these structures in place, they will rapidly disappear."

It is to help with this crisis that the Frank Lloyd Wright Building Conservancy exists. It is a partner to building owners helping them preserve and maintain the approximately 400 surviving Wright structures. The conservancy has forged a network of organizations and specialists who can offer professional expertise and technical assistance thereby sharing the burden of saving these vulnerable structures.

The conservancy is making a difference. Because of its efforts, buildings by Wright are standing that would otherwise have been lost.

In addition to helping owners locate specially qualified contractors, architects, and conservators, the conservancy provides publications and educational programs that address owners' specialized needs. It operates a real estate clearinghouse to link preservation-minded buyers with sellers of Wright properties. It helps homeowners to implement facade easements—legal devices that prevent future owners from destroying or defacing the property.

The conservancy also benefits hundreds of its members who are not themselves owners or administrators of Wright buildings. Members enjoy an annual conference highlighting successful preservation efforts, tours of private Wright homes, and the best of lecturers on Wright. They receive a stimulating, informative bulletin on Wright and help support publications such as this.

If you love Wright's work, then make a difference. Join the Frank Lloyd Wright Building Conservancy and participate in our programs.

Jonathan Lipman, AIA
President, The Frank Lloyd Wright Building Conservancy
Prairie Architects, Fairfield, Iowa

for information on membership, write or call:
Frank Lloyd Wright Building Conservancy
P.O. Box 5466
River Forest, IL 60305
(708) 848-1141

PREFACE

The sixty-six publicly accessible structures described in this guide range from office towers to bridges, from grand estates to homes for middle-Americans, from churches to barns, and even include a gas station and a windmill. Their forms and functions document the phenomenal diversity and ingenuity of Frank Lloyd Wright.

Some sites are historic house museums with extensive tour programs, others are functioning schools, churches, offices, and clinics that willingly accept visitors during regular business hours. This guide contains nearly all of the Wright-designed buildings in the United States and four international sites currently open to the public. Owners of the few sites not represented did not feel they could accommodate regular tour traffic at this time, but we hope to include them in future editions.

Before you visit, call in advance to confirm hours of operation, fees, and directions. Circumstances of ownership change, sites close for restoration, repair, and maintenance, and hours of operation may vary with the season. Many sites require reservations, and tours fill early, especially in the summer months. Travel itineraries, maps, and a list of archives are included at the back of the book.

The dates listed in this guide reflect the design of the structure and may not coincide with the period of construction nor year of completion. Symbols following the tour information for each entry indicate whether the site is accessible to the disabled, or if there is a restaurant, a book or gift shop, or an archive available to visitors. Directions are given from the closest major thoroughfare. Many sites are private homes; please respect the residential character of the neighborhoods. Park only in designated areas and remain on public walkways. Some sites restrict interior photography; please ask before taking photographs.

This second edition of *Wright Sites* includes twelve additional structures in the United States and four international sites, demonstrating the dedication of owners, site administrators, staff members, and volunteers to sharing the experience of

Wright's architecture with others. The Frank Lloyd Wright Building Conservancy gratefully acknowledges their central role in educating the public about the significance of Wright's life and work, and the importance of preserving these structures for future generations.

Many individuals have contributed their expertise, resources, and time to this publication, which would not have proceeded without the leadership and perseverance of past and present Conservancy presidents Carla Lind, Deborah Vick and Jonathan Lipman, AIA. Lipman and Jack Quinan have lent their considerable scholarly expertise to improving and revising the text. Photographs were generously lent by Bob Greenspan, Leo Holub, Don Kalec, Dave Karel, Jonathan Lipman, Jack Quinan, Robert Ruschak, Julius Shulman, Scot Zimmerman, and the Loomis Archive of the Mason City Public Library. With the assistance of The Frank Lloyd Wright Archives, we were able to reproduce original plans of several buildings.

Research assistance was provided by Margaret Klinkow, Frank Lloyd Wright Home and Studio Foundation Research Center, Yoshiko Koda, the Japan Information Center of the University of Pittsburgh, Mary Woolever, The Art Institute of Chicago Burnham Library, and Oscar Munoz and the staff of the Frank Lloyd Wright Archives. The assistance of Tom Schmidt and Vivian Loftness with access to the resources of the Carnegie Mellon University Library was greatly appreciated. Sara-Ann Briggs, Mary Jane Hamilton, Virgina Kazor, Pamela Kingsbury, Dixie Legler, Carla Lind, Robert McCoy, Tom Olsen, George Platt, Tony Puttnam, Catherine Voorsinger, and Ben Weese were among those whose own research or experience with specific sites greatly enhanced this publication.

Arlene Sanderson

INTRODUCTION

Frank Lloyd Wright's career in architecture began in 1887 and concluded in 1959, a seventy-two-year period of American history during which the country was transformed through technological and industrial developments and massive social change from a predominantly agrarian to a predominantly urban-industrial society. During that time, Wright designed more than 1,000 buildings, roughly 500 of which were built in more than 40 states, as well as in Canada and Japan. Approximately 400 of these buildings survive today; most are privately held, but 66 are accessible to the public as house museums or as functioning, tourable sites. *Wright Sites*, a catalog and guide to these publicly accessible structures, was produced by the Frank Lloyd Wright Building Conservancy to encourage and facilitate a public awareness of and visitations to the sites, and to promote the preservation of all existing Wright architecture.

Public appreciation of Wright's work has grown steadily since his death in 1959, and has accelerated dramatically during the past two decades owing to a cluster of intersecting forces. Among them is the failure of the Modern Movement in architecture, which began around 1910 in Europe, acknowledged Wright as a progenitor, eclipsed him in the 1930s, '40s, and '50s, and faded from view in the 1960s and '70s. Also significant in the resurgence of interest in Wright are the opening of his vast archives to researchers in the early 1980s, the emergence of an ecological consciousness in America—a movement that fits comfortably with Wright's deep regard for nature and the landscape—and the rampant proliferation of truly inferior buildings (merchandising markets, fast-food restaurants, and condominium complexes) on the American landscape, a phenomenon that fosters an appreciation, if not a hunger, for architecture of real quality. Last of all are the buildings, themselves, that yield layer upon layer of discovery and pleasure to those who live in them, study them, and visit them.

As a result of these conditions, the market has been flooded with publications on Wright; reproductions of his decorative designs are ubiquitous in museum shops and galleries; an opera has been written and produced on his life; a PBS series is in the works; videotapes and CD ROMS are available; exhibitions and symposia occur annually; and Wright has been returned to the curricula of most schools of architecture in America.

Most significant for our purposes, however, the number of Wright structures accessible to the public in the United States has risen from twenty-five to sixty-two in just ten years. Indeed, some critics are beginning to speak of Wright not only as America's greatest architect, but as one of the leading creative artists of western history, along with Michelangelo, Rembrandt, Mozart, and Beethoven. What lies behind this extravagant praise? Is the American view of Wright inflated for chauvinistic reasons, or is his work indeed worthy of such esteem?

The answers can be found in the buildings themselves, as we shall see, but some of the peripheral indicators of Wright's prodigious talent are worth considering. Wright is usually identified as an architect, but he was also a planner, an engineer, an author and lecturer, an accomplished musician, a social critic, a teacher, a farmer, an avid collector of Asian arts, a photographer, and a prolific designer of furniture and decorative arts. The archives of the Frank Lloyd Wright Foundation at Taliesin West, for example, contain 198,000 documents, including some 20,000 drawings representing primarily the *second half* of Wright's career (much of Wright's earlier work in the form of drawings and documents was lost to fire).

For many clients, Wright produced a full complement of furniture designs for the commission, each piece unique to the building. The Larkin Administration Building, for instance, included at least thirty-eight distinct designs—five different metal office chairs, five variations on the metal desk, three reclining lounge chairs, three wood and leather couches, four wooden chairs, seven different wooden tables, three varieties of lights, an umbrella stand, bookshelves, built-in file cabinets, a barrel chair, etc. Similarly, the Martin House contained more than thirty uniquely designed pieces of furniture. If these two buildings are representative, and if Wright furnished only one-fifth of his buildings, then he would have designed more than 2,000 pieces of furniture during his career. This rate of production is especially impressive when one considers that Wright spent most of his career working under considerable duress because he was not a good businessman and his personal life was often in disarray. In addition, for much of the period between 1910 and 1935, owing to personal misfortune and the Great Depression, Wright was hardly able to practice at all. In his final decade, from age 81 to 91, Wright produced six books, traveled widely in the United States and abroad, and produced as many buildings as he had in his previous sixty years!

Nevertheless, architecture, which Wright called "the mother of all the arts," remains central. Wright's architecture occurred in six phases across his career, any one of which would have gained him a distinguished place in American architectural history. His earliest work (see his Oak Park home, 1889) was somewhat derivative of the work of H.H. Richardson, Bruce Price, and McKim, Mead and White, leading architects of the 1880s whose work was widely published in periodicals. Wright's home resembles the shingled American modifications of the Queen Anne style, but its pinwheeling plan prefigures recurring spirals throughout Wright's career.

The second phase encompasses the 1890s and is classicizing in nature. Its strong if somewhat self-conscious buildings (see the Charnley House, 1891, and Wright's Oak Park studio and library, 1898) frequently include octagons or partial octagons, linear plans, and decorative evidences of Wright's five years under Louis Sullivan.

The third phase, the Prairie period, sometimes referred to as Wright's "First Golden Age," began in 1901 and extends into the 1910s. Here Wright created a distinctively American house type (see Dana House, 1902–04, Martin House, 1904, Robie House, 1906, May House, 1908), characterized by strong horizontality, cross-axial planning, low roofs with generous eaves protecting long sequences of art-glass windows, a natural use of materials, skeletal construction, broad openings between rooms, and close attention to the siting of the building on the landscape. The Prairie houses were the designs, along with the Larkin Administration Building and Unity Temple, that excited the European modernists. From 1901 to 1909, Wright produced Prairie houses at the rate of about twelve per year, including such renowned commissions as the Willits, Dana, Martin, Coonley, and Robie Houses.

Wright's interest in the decorative use of Mayan-inspired cast concrete began in the 1910s (see the German Warehouse, 1915) and culminated in the exotic textile block houses of the Los Angeles area (see the Barnsdall, 1919, Freeman, 1924, and Ennis, 1924, Houses), though Wright continued with a modified version of the concrete block design in his "Usonian Automatic" houses of the 1940s and '50s.

Wright's fifth and most productive period featured the Usonian house (see the Rosenbaum, 1939, Pope, 1940, and Affleck, 1940, Houses), a lower-cost house type than the Prairie house. The Usonians had a heated concrete floor slab, sandwich wall construction, simplified plan types such as the L-shape and the in-line, and extensive use of built-in furniture, often in plywood. Wright also created more elaborate houses during this period (see the Hanna House, 1936) using hexagonal modules and plans based upon triangles, circles, or hemicircles.

Finally, there are buildings from throughout Wright's career, usually large-scale, non-domestic commissions that are distinguished by the boldness of their conception and the innovativeness of their engineering. These include several extraordinary but demolished structures: the Larkin Administration Building, 1904, Midway Gardens, 1914, and the Imperial Hotel, 1915–22, as well as a substantial number of publicly accessible buildings (see Unity Temple, 1905, the S.C. Johnson Wax Company headquarters, 1936, Florida Southern University, 1938–1954, the Price Tower, 1952, the Solomon R. Guggenheim Museum, 1956, Marin County Civic Center, 1957, Grady Gammage Memorial Auditorium, 1959).

All of Wright's work, from the humblest Usonian to the most elaborate Prairie house, is conceived around an idea or grand motif that is expressive of the building's function, its client, and its site, disciplined by elemental geometry. In some instances, such as the "Hollyhock" House or "Fallingwater," Wright's title is a clue to the theme of the building.

There is also good evidence that Wright's manner of creating his buildings was akin to that of the great composers. Indeed, he told one client that he would give him a "domestic symphony," and therein lies the source of endless fascination in Wright's work. The Frank Lloyd Wright Building Conservancy does not promote and defend Wright's architecture merely because he was prolific and innovative, but because these structures were conceived and developed so thoroughly, with such consistency of principle and careful interrelationship of part to part and part to whole as to constitute a composition or thematized system of symphonic pretension, endlessly rewarding to those who wish to engage them.

While it is somewhat unfashionable to rave about genius in this postmodern era—the word genius is over-used and does not signify anything specific in terms of accomplishment—the fact is that Frank Lloyd Wright created numerous buildings that have elevated architecture to the highest level of artistic achievement, and sixty-six of these structures are yours to discover.

Jack Quinan
Professor of Art History
State University of New York, Buffalo

SITES

STANLEY AND MILDRED ROSENBAUM HOUSE

"The house of moderate cost is not only America's major architectural problem but the problem most difficult for her major architects," Frank Lloyd Wright wrote in 1943. Wright spent much of the latter part of his career answering that challenge in various designs of the Usonian house. Among these functional, cost-effective Usonians (a loosely construed acronym for United States of America) was the Rosenbaum House, a 1540-square-foot residence built at a cost of $12,000.

By eliminating the basement and attic, embedding heating pipes in a concrete floor mat, centralizing the mechanical systems and plumbing near the workplace/kitchen, and building in furnishings and lighting, Wright intended to develop a simpler, more efficient house suited to the informality of middle-American family life. His concept anticipated the prefabrication of major components. The walls, for example, were designed with a plywood core sandwiched between board-and-batten interior and exterior surfaces. Conventional framing, plaster, and paint were thus eliminated.

A very pure example of the Usonian type, the Rosenbaum House was originally designed as an L-shaped plan on a two-by-four-foot grid. The large living room included an asymmetrically positioned fireplace and dining alcove at one end and a 100-square-foot study at the other. The bedroom wing provided access to three rooms off a long, narrow gallery lined with

1939

ADDRESS
601 Riverview Drive
Florence, Alabama 35630
(205) 764-5274

ACCESS
Guided tours by appointment only.
Adults $5, seniors and students $4.
No children under age 6.

DIRECTIONS
Take I-65 to U.S. Highway 72.
Travel west to Court Street. Turn left continuing on to Dr. Hicks Boulevard. Turn left and continue west to Riverview Drive.

bookshelves and storage. In 1948, Wright designed a significant addition to the house, providing a larger kitchen, a playroom, and guest quarters that wrap three sides of a landscaped courtyard.

Red brick from northern Alabama clay, and Southern cypress combine to establish a nearly solid wall on the street side of the house. The twenty-foot-long cantilevered carport reinforces the house's emphatic horizontal profile. By contrast, the rear of the house is remarkably open, with floor-to-ceiling windows and doors opening to the terrace, a Japanese garden, and the woods beyond.

The fretwork ply-wood panels framing the clerestory windows and concealing recessed lights are typical of Usonian houses and are consistent with Wright's philosophy of integral ornament. The Wright-designed furnishings are supplemented by stock pieces by the noted designer Charles Eames.

ARIZONA BILTMORE HOTEL AND COTTAGES

The Arizona Biltmore Hotel and Cottage complex is generally recognized as a collaboration between Frank Lloyd Wright and Albert Chase McArthur, a former draftsman in Wright's Oak Park studio. The precise extent of Wright's involvement remains unclear. McArthur's signature appears on drawings for the project, and he was responsible for the general plan of the hotel. He called on Wright for technical assistance with the design and engineering of the buildings' concrete block system, as Wright had experimented with the use of cast concrete blocks joined with metal rods in the design of several Los Angeles houses, and published the results in a 1927 issue of *Architectural Record*.

Wright was paid $10,000 for rights to use the block system. He spent the first five months of 1928 working in Phoenix with McArthur, so refinements of the plans during this period were likely his own; he was paid an additional $1,000 for six drawings. The Biltmore could have demonstrated the structural ingenuity and economy of the concrete block system when used on a grand scale, but contractors unwilling to trust Wright's innovations insisted on using more conventional methods of construction in combination with the block system.

1927

ADDRESS
24th Street and Missouri Avenue
Phoenix, Arizona 85016
(602) 954-7000

ACCESS
Guided tours by appointment; call
for reservations. $15

DIRECTIONS
Travel north on I-17 (Black Canyon
Freeway) to Missouri Avenue. Turn
right and continue to 24th Street.

The hotel complex sits on 200 acres of a proposed 621-acre development. An entrance wing projects from the main four-story block, which contains the lobby, dining room, and sun room on the first floor with guest rooms on the upper levels. The drama of the lobby is enhanced by the second-floor balcony and the ceiling covered with gold leaf, and the concrete floor is incised with a grid corresponding to the dimensions of the unit blocks. A polygonal ballroom occupies one of the two wings that extend to the rear of the hotel and partially enclose a hexagonal patio. Fifteen guest cottages were constructed behind the main building.

When the stock market crashed, the hotel was sold to the Wrigley chewing gum family, stockholders in the venture. In 1973, the building was sold again, just before a construction-related fire destroyed the entire fourth floor and copper roof. Taliesin Architects supervised the reconstruction and restoration, and original drawings were used to reproduce the interiors.

More recently, the 500-room luxury resort was remodeled in a $35-million project that included the construction of a pool complex, a pavilion, a 16,000-square-foot multi-use center, and an 18-hole championship putting course, as well as the renovation of the lobby and the modernization of the guest rooms.

FIRST CHRISTIAN CHURCH

1950

ADDRESS
6750 North Seventh Avenue
Phoenix, Arizona 85013
(602) 246-9206

ACCESS
Free guided tours by appointment
only, Mon–Fri, 8:30 AM–5 PM.

DIRECTIONS
Take I-17 east (Black Canyon
Freeway) to Seventh Avenue.
Turn right on Seventh Avenue
and go two blocks to church.

Frank Lloyd Wright's design for the First Christian Church reflects his belief that the modern church should be a building without historical or sectarian reference. The triangle, symbolizing the Christian Trinity, is essential to the concept and form of this structure. Twenty-three triangular, steel and concrete pillars support the building. The pyramidal roof and a seventy-seven-foot spire crown a second, narrower range of triangular columns that frame clerestory windows. Light filters through the spire's colored glass insets onto the floor of the diamond-shaped sanctuary. The church's 120-foot bell tower has four unequal sides, giving the free-standing structure a triangular appearance.

Completed in 1972, thirteen years after Wright's death, the church sanctuary was originally designed as a university chapel for Southwest Christian Seminary. Peyton Canary, the seminary president, had commissioned the design in 1949, along with administrative and lecture facilities, a library, a Greek theater, and faculty housing for a proposed eighty-acre campus. The university was never built, but in 1970, members of the First Christian congregation approached the Frank Lloyd Wright Foundation about reviving the 1950 plan for their new church.

The sanctuary of the steel, concrete, and native stone structure seats 1,000. The addition of a baptistry and choir loft were the only modifications to Wright's design. In 1979, the congregation added an administrative wing by Taliesin Architects.

TALIESIN WEST

1937

ADDRESS
12621 N. Frank Lloyd Wright
Boulevard
Scottsdale, Arizona 85261-4430
(602) 860-8810

ACCESS
Guided, one-hour tours daily.
Oct–May: 9 AM–4 PM. Adults $10,
seniors and students $8, children
ages 4 to 12 $3.
June–Sept: 8–11 AM.
Adults $8, seniors and students $6,
children ages 4 to 12 $3.

Behind-the-Scenes Tour.
Oct–May: Thurs, 9 AM–noon.
Jan–May: Tues/Thurs 9 AM–noon.
$25 per person, reservations
recommended.

Guided Desert Walk.
Nov–April: Mon–Sat 11:15 AM and
2:15 PM.
$12.

Night Lights on the Desert.
March–May: Wed 7 –9 PM.
$25 per person, reservations
recommended.

Call (602) 860-2700 for group tour
information.

DIRECTIONS
In northeast Scottsdale near Shea
Boulevard and 114th Street.

In 1937, Frank Lloyd Wright purchased 600 acres of rugged land in the Sonoran Desert at the foot of the McDowell Mountains. He established an experimental desert camp that would serve as his winter home, studio, and architectural laboratory until his death in 1959. Over the years, the quarter-mile complex was continually altered and expanded to comprise a drafting studio, Wright's office and private living quarters, dining facilities, three theaters, and a workshop, as well as residences for apprentices and staff, all situated among pools, terraces, and gardens.

Constructed of stone, cement, redwood, and canvas, the buildings seem to grow out of the desert terrain that inspired their design. Their angled roofs, exposed beams, and rubble walls mirror the colors, textures, and forms of the surrounding landscape. As the buildings took on greater permanence, steel and fiberglass replaced the less durable materials.

The ninety-six-by-thirty-foot drafting room with a fireplace and "desert-masonry" vault, and a communal dining room and two apartments, form the core of the complex. An adjoining terrace leads to the fifty-six-foot-long garden room with a sloping, translucent roof and a fireplace. Wright's private quarters were located in the wing extending at a ninety-degree angle to the southeast. Additional structures (the Cabaret Theater and a larger pavilion for live performances, concerts and lectures) were designed to house social and cultural activities integrated into the educational program of the

Taliesin Fellowship and Frank Lloyd Wright School of Architecture. Wright had founded both to train future architects by emphasizing hands-on experience. Apprentices live in apartments on the site, as well as in "tents" of their own design scattered throughout the surrounding desert.

Taliesin West is the international headquarters of the Frank Lloyd Wright Foundation. The foundation owns and manages Taliesin (Spring Green, Wisconsin), Taliesin West, the Frank Lloyd Wright Archive, an accredited architectural school, and Taliesin Architects, a for-profit subsidiary and the successor to Wright's architecture and design firm. The archive contains 22,000 original drawings and more than 400,000 other items related to Wright's work and life. An international

resource for museums, scholars, and researchers, the archives are accessible by writing the Director of Archives at Taliesin West.

Taliesin West is one of seventeen structures designed by Wright to earn special recognition from the American Institute of Architects as representative of his contribution to American culture.

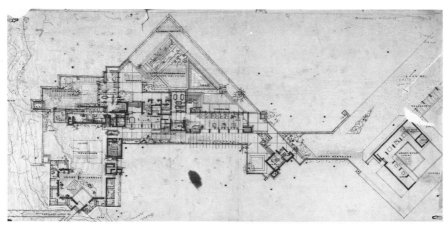

GRADY GAMMAGE MEMORIAL AUDITORIUM

During the last year of his life, Frank Lloyd Wright received his only civic commission from the state of Arizona, where he lived during the winter months. This final public space of Wright's design is a circular, 3,000-seat center for the performing arts with a concert hall, proscenium theater, classrooms, and offices.

The building was commissioned by Grady Gammage, the University's ninth president and a long-time friend of the architect. The fifteen-acre site on the southwest corner of the campus was formerly a women's athletic field. Wright designed two, 200-foot-long pedestrian bridges that rise from the adjacent lawn and sunken parking area to the circular building. Constructed of steel, cast concrete, and brick, the building cost $2.5 million.

An arcade of fifty 55-foot-long columns wraps the facade, framing the glass-walled lobby and supporting the outer edge of the thin-shell concrete roof. The plan is divided into two circles of unequal size. The larger contains the promenades, lobbies, and audience hall; the smaller, the stage, dressing rooms, workshops, classrooms, and offices.

The continental-style seating in the auditorium eliminates radial aisles: patrons enter and exit through twenty-four doors along the side and rear of the room. A grand tier and balcony provide upper-level seating. The grand tier is supported by a 145-foot-long girder

1959

ADDRESS
Arizona State University
Apache Boulevard at Mill Avenue
Tempe, Arizona 85287-0105
(602) 965-4050

ACCESS
Free guided tours Mon–Fri, 1–3:30
PM. *No tours during scheduled*
performances or on holidays.

DIRECTIONS
From I-10, exit at Broadway East
and continue for two miles to Mill
Avenue. Turn left and continue
traveling north, passing 13th Street.
Turn left at curve to remain on
Mill Avenue. Continue north to
Gammage Parkway and turn right.

and is detached from the rear wall, allowing sound to encircle the audience.

The 140-foot-wide stage is a multipurpose performing space, readily adapted for a wide range of theatrical productions, symphony concerts, chamber music recitals, and lectures. The steel acoustical shell can be mechanically adjusted to accommodate a full symphony orchestra and choir, or collapsed against the rear wall.

Neither Wright nor Gammage lived to see the building completed in 1964. William Wesley Peters of Taliesin Architects was responsible for the engineering and much of the interior design of the building.

ANDERTON COURT SHOPS

1952

ADDRESS
332 N. Rodeo Drive
Beverly Hills, California 90210

ACCESS
No organized tour program.
Shops open Mon–Sat, 10 AM–6 PM.

DIRECTIONS
From the San Diego Freeway (405)
exit east at Santa Monica
Boulevard and continue into
Beverly Hills. Travel south on
Rodeo Drive for three blocks.

To maximize usable floor space on this prime piece of real estate, Frank Lloyd Wright organized a series of small boutiques vertically around a central light well. The top floor was planned for use as an apartment with a small penthouse. A narrow, angled ramp provides access to the upper-level shops. A central stylized pylon reaches well beyond the rooftop, commanding the attention of street traffic. The canopy and signage are later additions inconsistent with Wright's design.

ALINE BARNSDALL HOUSE

1919

ADDRESS
Hollyhock House
4808 Hollywood Boulevard
Los Angeles, California 90027
(213) 662-7272

ACCESS
Guided tours Tues–Sun: noon, 1, 2,
and 3 PM.
Adults $2, seniors $1, children
under age 12 free.
Foreign language tours by special
arrangement. Groups of fifteen
or more by appointment only; call
(213) 485-4581.

DIRECTIONS
From Hollywood Freeway, take
either Hollywood Boulevard or
Vermont Avenue exit. Entrance to
Barnsdall Art Park is on Hollywood
Boulevard, one block west of
Vermont Avenue.

Frank Lloyd Wright described the large and enigmatic house he designed for oil heiress and theatrical producer Aline Barnsdall as a "California Romanza." "I feel in the silhouette of the Olive Hills house [Hollyhock House] a sense of the breadth of the romance of the region." Variously described as Mayan, pre-Columbian, Asian, and even Egyptian, Hollyhock House defies stylistic categorization. It is a transitional structure, a bridge between the Prairie houses of the preceding decades and the textile block houses to come.

Barnsdall had been introduced to Wright in Chicago, where she first considered building a theater of his design. Her plans changed, and she purchased a thirty-six-acre hilltop site in east Hollywood. She commissioned Wright to design an elaborate complex of residences, theaters, shops, and apartments to serve a Los Angeles community of avant-garde artists. Hollyhock House (Barnsdall's private residence), two guest residences, and a spring house were the only buildings completed of the extensive program. A fourth structure, known as the "Little Dipper," was begun but never completed; its retaining walls remain.

Plans to construct the house of reinforced concrete were abandoned in the drawing stage, and construction proceeded in hollow tile, stucco, and wood. Hollyhocks, Barnsdall's favorite flower, inspired the stylized, cast concrete, ornamental bands on the exterior walls, as well as the capitals on the courtyard piers and the finials projecting from the roof.

The quadrangular plan encloses a large garden court that terminates in a circular pool. The central block of the house comprises an entry loggia and a living room, which is flanked by a library and a music room. Two opposing wings, which extend from the main living area, contain the bedrooms, dining room, and service areas of the home. The living room is distinguished by a central fireplace with

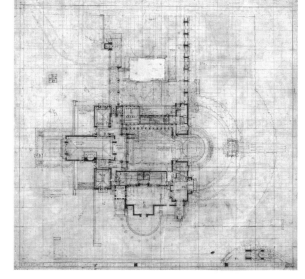

a decorative overmantel and projecting hearth surrounded by a pool of water. The large, sculptural forms of the complex seating group designed by Wright create an intimate space within the larger room. Barnsdall's wish for a residence that was half house and half garden is answered in numerous terraces, colonnades, and pergolas that join the interior spaces with the garden.

Barnsdall's peripatetic lifestyle and disappointment at a house too large and a cost too great eventually resulted in her abandoning Hollyhock House. She preferred to stay in one of the smaller Wright-designed residences on the site. In 1927, Barnsdall donated Hollyhock House, one of the guest residences, and eleven acres of what is now Barnsdall Art Park to the City of Los Angeles. In 1974, Lloyd Wright, Frank Lloyd Wright's son, directed a restoration of the house. In 1991, the massive living room seating group was reconstructed using historic photographs.

The Barnsdall House is one of seventeen structures designed by Wright to earn special recognition from the American Institute of Architects as representative of his contribution to American culture.

CHARLES AND MABEL ENNIS HOUSE

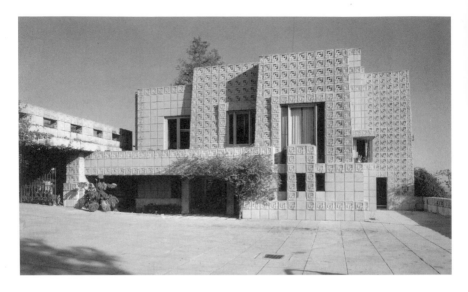

Frank Lloyd Wright had been experimenting with the potential of precast concrete block for more than a decade when in the 1920s, he adopted the material and method for the design of several California projects. The medium promised economy, and the blocks could be fashioned from readily available local materials. When cast in patterned molds, the blocks became both decorative and structural, and could serve both as finished exterior and interior surfaces in the building.

The house Charles and Mabel Ennis commissioned in 1923 for a half-acre site in the Hollywood Hills is the largest and last of Wright's Los Angeles concrete-block dwellings. Constructed of sixteen-inch square blocks joined with metal reinforcing rods, the building rises in stages from an enormous platform buttressed by a retaining wall. The division of the facade in zones of smooth and patterned blocks continues on the interior walls. Geometric patterns in the art-glass windows recall Wright's earlier designs for Prairie houses. The wisteria motif also appears in the glass tile mosaic above the living room fireplace.

The entry hall is a low, long, and dark passageway below the main living area. The upper level, by contrast, seems enormous, with ceiling heights reaching twenty-two feet. A 100-foot-long loggia extends across the front of the house, connecting the main living areas—dining and living rooms—with the two bedrooms.

1924

ADDRESS
Ennis-Brown House
2655 Glendower Avenue
Los Angeles, California 90027-1114
(213) 660-0607

ACCESS
Guided public tours on second Sat of Jan, March, May, July, Sept, Nov.
Adults $10, seniors, students, and children $5 (children in arms free). Tours for schools, architectural groups, and out-of-town visitors $10 per person.
All tours by reservation only.

DIRECTIONS
Exit I-5 (Golden State Freeway) at Los Feliz Boulevard West.
Continue west to Vermont Avenue. Turn right on Vermont and left at Cromwell. Cross center divider strip to stop sign at Glendower Avenue. Turn right and continue up hill.

As was the case with Wright's other concrete block houses in Los Angeles, construction was supervised by his son, Lloyd Wright. In 1940, the house was sold to John Nesbitt, a radio personality. Nesbitt added a swimming pool and billiard room of Wright's design, but the furnishing designs he commissioned from the architect were never executed. Since 1980, the house has been owned by the Trust for Preservation of Cultural Heritage, a non-profit, public-benefit corporation.

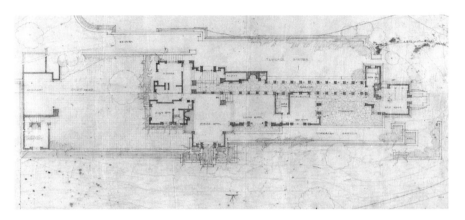

SAMUEL AND HARRIET FREEMAN HOUSE

Sam and Harriet Freeman were newly married members of Los Angeles's artistic avant-garde when they first encountered Frank Lloyd Wright's architecture at Hollyhock House, the home of theatrical producer Aline Barnsdall. When the Freemans asked Wright to design a house for $10,000, he seized the opportunity to use the textile block system of construction. Wright claimed the system promised affordability through the use of inexpensive materials, on-site modular fabrication, and assembly by unskilled laborers. In actuality, when completed the house cost $23,000.

The walls are constructed of some 12,000 sixteen-inch-square concrete blocks, cast on site and joined with metal reinforcing rods. The mold imparts both pattern and texture to the surface of the blocks. When joined, the combinations of solid, perforated, and patterned blocks contribute to a unified decorative scheme that extends throughout the house on both interior and exterior aspects. In addition, light passing through the perforated blocks creates flickering patterns of light and shadow on interior surfaces.

1924

ADDRESS
1962 Glencoe Way
Los Angeles, California 90068
(213) 851-0671

ACCESS
Guided tours: Sat 2 and 4 PM.
Closed on national holidays.
Adults $10, students $5.

DIRECTIONS
Exit Hollywood Freeway (101) at Highland. Proceed south to Franklin (approximately three blocks). Park at Methodist Church lot, Highland and Franklin. Walk up Hillcrest (one block west of Highland) to Glencoe. Continue one-half block up Glencoe to house.

The plan exploits the steep and narrow lot over-looking Hollywood. The building appears to be a single story from the street, but actually extends down the slope an additional two levels. Large areas of glass and the inventive use of mitered glass at a corner window serve to visually expand the modest-sized though dramatic interior. A balcony extends the main living area, while the lower-level bedrooms open onto a terrace.

The dwelling incorporates the openness and central hearth of the earlier Prairie houses, the extensive ornamental potential of the textile blocks, and traces of Japanese, Mayan, and European modern inspiration. Wright designed few furnishings for the Freemans, which were soon replaced by designs of Rudolph Schindler, a Viennese architect who studied briefly at Taliesin and moved to Los Angeles under Wright's employ. As an independent designer, Schindler played a pivotal role in the transformation of Southern California architecture, and the Freemans turned to the younger architect for modifications of their house.

Upon Harriet Freeman's death in 1986, the house became the property of the University of Southern California, whose school of architecture is responsible for the building's restoration and maintenance.

V.C. MORRIS GIFT SHOP

Frank Lloyd Wright rejected all conventions of ground-level display windows for retail establishments in his design of a gift shop for California businessman V.C. Morris. The street side of this undistinguished city lot is completely encompassed by an imposing masonry facade. The solid brick curtain wall that rises dramatically from the street is pierced by two slender strands of illuminated glass converging at the impressive arched opening and barrel-vaulted entryway. The composition is an elegantly conceived interplay of solid and void, light and shadow, angle and curve. The monumental masonry arch recalls the influence of Louis Sullivan, Wright's early employer and teacher, about whom Wright wrote the biography, *Genius and the Mobocracy*, in 1948.

Wright intended the mysterious reticence of the facade to entice passersby through the tunnel-like entrance to the interior, which is an expansive, light-filled space, well-suited to the display of art or decorative wares. A curvilinear ramp leads to the upper level and provides additional display area along its length. The ramp walls contain circular recesses for the display of art, as well as openings that provide a view through to the other levels of the store. The curvilinear theme extends to the design of display cases, tables, seating, and built-in cabinetry, all of black walnut.

1948

ADDRESS
Circle Gallery (currently)
140 Maiden Lane
San Francisco, California 94108
(415) 989-2100

ACCESS
No organized tours.
Open during business hours:
Mon–Sat, 10 AM–6 PM; Sun,
noon–5 PM.
Groups of ten or more by
appointment only.
Site available for special-use rental
by corporate and not-for-profit
organizations.

DIRECTIONS
Located in downtown San
Francisco's Union Square, between
Stockton and Grant Streets.

Similarities between the design of the store and concurrent work on plans for the Guggenheim Museum are obvious. Less well-known was an earlier unexecuted design for Morris of a spectacular, cylindrical, cliffside house whose three tiers were accessible by a series of ramps.

A retail space until 1983, the building now houses a gallery of contemporary art. The building is one of seventeen structures designed by Wright to earn special recognition from the American Institute of Architects as representative of his contribution to American culture.

MARIN COUNTY CIVIC CENTER

The Marin County Board of Supervisors purchased 140 acres north of San Rafael, intending to centralize under one roof thirteen widely dispersed county departments. They commissioned Frank Lloyd Wright to develop a master plan for the site. In 1957, he presented a design for the Administration Building and the Hall of Justice, followed by preliminary plans for a theater, an auditorium, a fairground pavilion, and a lagoon. Construction had just begun at the time of Wright's death in 1959; William Wesley Peters of Taliesin and Aaron Green, a San Francisco architect and Wright associate, became the project directors.

Wright's plan specified a 584-foot-long Administration Building and an 880-foot-long Hall of Justice that would bridge the valleys between three adjacent hills. The focal point and center of the plan was a flattened dome, eighty feet in diameter, crowned by a 172-foot gold tower encasing a smokestack. The Administration Building houses offices as well as a domed, circular county library and the Anne T. Kent California History Room. The Hall of Justice, completed in 1969, contains circular courtrooms, offices, a cafe, and the original county jail.

1957

ADDRESS
North San Pedro Road at U.S. 101
San Rafael, California
(415) 499-7407

MAILING ADDRESS
3501 Civic Center Drive
San Rafael, CA 94903

ACCESS
Building hours: 9 AM–4 PM.
Free one-hour guided tour:
Tues–Fri 10:30 AM.
Meet at second-floor gift shop in
Hall of Justice. Group and other
tours by appointment only, $1 per
person. Call (415) 472-7470.

DIRECTIONS
From San Francisco, take U.S. 101
to North San Pedro Road east.
Turn left at first stop light (Civic
Center Drive). Turn left again
immediately and continue toward
archway under county building.

The buildings were constructed of precast, prestressed concrete and steel at a cost of $16.7 million. Segmentation and the use of expansion joints allows the buildings to withstand seismic shock. Wright planned the central atriums to be open to the sky, but practical considerations prompted a change to barrel-vaulted skylights after his death. The exterior screen walls are divided into rhythmic arcades and circular openings that shade the buildings' interior while framing views of the surrounding hills. The circular motif is continued in the grillwork and gold-anodized aluminum spheres rimming the roof edge.

The site includes a circular post office, Wright's only commission for a U.S. government facility. Later construction includes the Veterans' Memorial Auditorium, an exhibition hall, fairgrounds, and a maintenance facility. Native plants and a fourteen-acre lagoon with an island are featured in the landscape design.

PAUL R. AND JEAN S. HANNA HOUSE

This house, designed for a Stanford University professor and his young family, exemplifies Frank Lloyd Wright's endless exploration and innovation as he resisted the "pull of the specious old box." For the first time, abandoning the square or rectangle in favor of the hexagon as a basic unit for the grid and plan, Wright found a new freedom that translated into a remarkable degree of flexibility and spatial continuity. Walls joined at 120-degree obtuse angles create an interior of fluid space and unrestricted views, further extended by large expanses of glass that open out to the terraces and hillside.

The house, which even in its initial design greatly exceeded the Hannas' proposed budget of $15,000, grew through successive additions to encompass 4,825 square feet. In 1950 the Hannas added a wing, separated from the main house by the carport, that included guest quarters and a workshop. In 1957 they again turned to Wright, asking him to remodel the three children's bedrooms into a new master bedroom and to convert the parents' room into a library/office.

While generally considered a Usonian, the eventual size and cost of this dwelling far surpassed the means of the typical "middle American." But the reliance on a grid in the development of the plan, interior and exterior board-and-batten walls, and central location of the

1936

ADDRESS
Stanford, California

MAILING ADDRESS
*Stanford University Museum of Art
Stanford, CA 94305-5060*

ACCESS
Temporarily closed due to earthquake damage sustained in 1989. Will re-open when extensive structural repairs are completed.

kitchen are characteristics shared with Wright's Usonian designs elsewhere.

The Hannas' published correspondence with the architect demonstrates their shared commitment to achieving a house that would respond to the changing needs of family life while embodying Wright's principles of organic design. This partnership challenged the resources of architect and client alike to produce a dwelling of enduring appeal. The Hanna House is one of seventeen structures designed by Wright to earn special recognition from the American Institute of Architects as representative of his contribution to American culture.

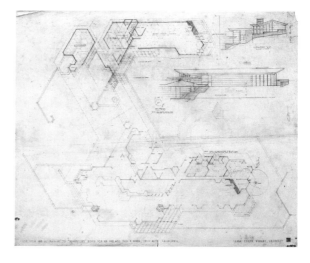

FLORIDA SOUTHERN UNIVERSITY

On land once occupied by a citrus grove, Frank Lloyd Wright set out to design a "truly American campus." In 1938, Dr. Ludd Spivey, president of Florida Southern College from 1925 to 1957, commissioned Wright to produce a master plan for the lakeside campus of this small, Methodist school. Spivey envisioned a chapel, library, administration building, faculty housing, dormitories, classrooms, industrial arts building, music building, science and cosmography building, and an art gallery with studio-workshops.

Over the next twenty years, buildings of Wright's design took form, beginning in 1938 with the hexagonal Annie Pfeiffer Chapel, which is both the tallest building of the complex and the focal point of the plan. The chapel's angular, vertical silhouette provides a strong visual counterpoint to the low, flat-roofed, rectangular seminar buildings of 1940 and the circular reading room of the original Roux Library completed in 1945. Other Wright-designed structures are the Watson Administration Building, actually two buildings separated by a courtyard containing a reflecting pool and

1938

ADDRESS
111 Lake Hollingsworth Drive
Lakeland, Florida 33801
(813) 680-4116

ACCESS
Free self-guided walking tour with map available at Watson Administration Building. Guided group tours by appointment only, $5 per person.

DIRECTIONS
From I-4, exit at Highway 37 and go south to McDonald. Turn left and continue straight ahead to the campus.

connected by an esplanade; the Ordway Building, with interior courtyards and a circular theater; the small Danforth Chapel; and the three-story Polk County Science Building, which contains the only planetarium of Wright's design.

The walls and structural members of the buildings are uniformly constructed of tan-colored, reinforced cast concrete. Wright's philosophy of integral ornament is demonstrated in his reliance on contrasting surfaces of smooth, textured, and perforated block, and abstract patterns of colored glass set into the concrete for decorative effect. Wright intended the trellises that extend from the copper-trimmed roofs to support trailing vines. Covered esplanades link this exceptionally large collection of Wright-designed buildings. The light wells and large planters of these flat-roofed walkways, in addition to the trees preserved from the original grove, create a garden-like setting on the eighty-acre site.

W.H. PETTIT MEMORIAL CHAPEL

Emma Glasner Pettit commissioned Frank Lloyd Wright to design a chapel for the Belvidere Cemetery, eighty miles northwest of Chicago, as a memorial to her husband, William H. Pettit, M.D. At the time of his death in 1899, Pettit lived and practiced in Cedar Falls, Iowa, but he had grown up in Belvidere.

This small, chaste, Prairie-period structure could be used for services and sheltered visitors during inclement weather. The cruciform plan of the building terminates in lateral porches providing protected access and extending the usable space. Features typical of Wright's Prairie designs include the low, hipped roof, broad eaves, bands of art-glass windows, horizontal wood trim, and the central brick fireplace. Spindle-backed wooden folding chairs were arranged facing the hearth.

The stucco building, which cost $3,000 to construct, was restored in 1981 with $56,000 in funds raised by the local Junior Woman's Club. The windows were recreated from original drawings and photographs, and the light fixtures and ceiling trim were inspired by similar Wright designs of the period.

1906

ADDRESS
North Main at Harrison
Belvidere, Illinois 61008
(815) 547-7642

ACCESS
No organized tours.
Cemetery hours: Mon–Fri
8 AM–noon, 1–4 PM.
Groups of ten or more by
appointment only.

DIRECTIONS
From I-90, exit at Genoa Road and turn right. Continue to third light and turn left on Route 76. Go straight ahead to cemetery.

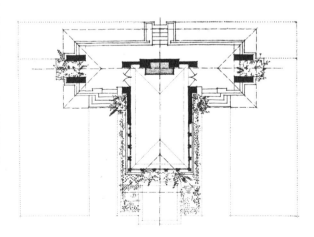

JAMES AND HELEN CHARNLEY HOUSE

1891

ADDRESS
Charnley-Persky House (currently)
Society of Architectural Historians
1365 North Astor Street
Chicago, Illinois 60610
(312) 573-1365

ACCESS
Open for tours on limited basis.
Call for information.

DIRECTIONS
Take Lake Shore Drive north to
North Avenue exit. Follow Inner
Drive and go south (left) to Astor
Street. Turn right to 1365 North
Astor.

Frank Lloyd Wright was the twenty-four-year-old chief draftsman in the office of Dankmar Adler and Louis Sullivan when James Charnley commissioned the design of this house. The firm specialized in large commercial structures, and smaller residential commissions were often assigned to Wright. Sullivan, a personal friend of the Charnleys, probably reviewed Wright's drawings, and the house is the product of their collaboration. A similar division of work roles probably prevailed in 1890, when Wright designed vacation bungalows for both Sullivan and the Charnleys in Ocean Springs, Mississippi.

In the design of this building, Wright said he first recognized the decorative value of the plain surface. The uncompromising simplicity, boldly stated geometry, and decorative restraint of the building's exterior distinguished it from other turn-of-the-century residences in this prestigious Chicago neighborhood. The facade is divided into three clearly differentiated, interlocking parts: the dressed-stone base extends to frame the entrance, the two-story block of Roman brick recedes to frame a central loggia, and a thin stringcourse of contrasting stone delineates the attic floor.

The interior plan is equally straightforward. A dramatic, open stair-hall rises three floors to a central skylight. The large entrance hall dominates the center of the first-floor space with the living and dining rooms on opposite ends. Bedrooms were located on the second floor, servants' quarters on the third, and the kitchen in the basement. Sullivan's influence is noticeable in the decorative detailing on the wood trim throughout the house.

The building, restored by Skidmore Owings and Merrill in 1988, serves as the national headquarters of the Society of Architectural Historians.

FREDERICK C. AND LORA H. ROBIE HOUSE

The Robie House remains Frank Lloyd Wright's consummate Prairie style house adapted to an urban site. An imposing presence in this neighborhood of large turn-of-the-century houses and eclectic university buildings, the long, low dwelling with its dramatic twenty-foot cantilevered terrace roofs still seems a structural marvel.

Robie was among the Midwestern clients who Wright described as men "with unspoiled instincts and untainted ideals." A successful bicycle manufacturer, he was also an engineer and an aspiring automotive designer. According to Robie, he sketched his own idea of what a house should be and passed the design among a few builders. "You want one of those damn Wright houses," he was told.

The house Wright designed both satisfied his client and fully integrated the design elements developed in earlier Prairie residences. Wright eliminated the basement and set the building on a concrete watertable. Brick piers and steel beams provide the structural framework upon which the three graduated tiers of the house rest. The low hipped roof with its wide and projecting eaves, and the narrow brick with raked, horizontal mortar joints all reinforce the dominant horizontality of the building.

Lacking sufficient ground for a garden, Wright carried the landscaping aloft in massive planters and urns, whose trailing foliage softened the dense mass of the exterior walls. At each level, doors and windows opened onto terraces, balconies, or porches, extending the living space out into nature.

1906

ADDRESS
5757 S. Woodlawn Avenue
Chicago, Illinois 60637
(312) 702-2150

ACCESS
Guided tours daily at noon.
Closed major holidays.
Adults $3, seniors and students $1,
children under age 10 free.
Groups of ten of more by appointment only. $15 guide fee plus $2
per person. Call (312) 702-8374 for
information.

DIRECTIONS
From I-90/94, take I-55 East exit.
Exit onto Lake Shore Drive South
and continue to 53rd Street. Turn
right and continue to Woodlawn
Avenue. Turn left. Limited street
parking available.

The entrance is concealed on the north side of the building. The first floor contained a playroom, a billiard room, and an attached garage. Robie shared Wright's fascination with the automobile, which may explain the three-car garage outfitted with an engine pit and car wash. The main living area is located on the second floor; the long, open expanse of space on this level is interrupted only by the fireplace block separating the dining and living room areas. The third-floor bedrooms include a master suite with a fireplace and bath.

Wright designed the house in its entirety, enriching the interior with furnishings, light fixtures, rugs, and art glass. The house, including the lot, cost Robie $59,000, a considerable sum at the time. The sale of the house in 1911, just two years after completion, coincided with the failure of Robie's marriage and business. In 1957, the building was saved from demolition by a realty company that later transferred ownership to the University of Chicago.

A National Historic Landmark, the Robie House is one of seventeen structures designed by Wright to earn special recognition from the American Institute of Architects as representative of his contribution to American culture.

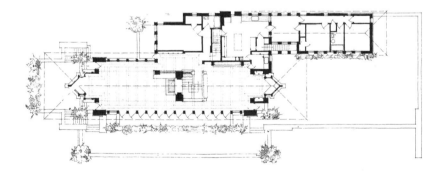

ROOKERY BUILDING ENTRY LOBBY REMODELING

ADDRESS
LaSalle and Adams Streets
Chicago, Illinois 60604

ACCESS
No organized tours.
Building hours: Mon–Fri,
8 AM–6 PM.

DIRECTIONS
Take I-290 east to downtown
Chicago. Exit at Franklin Street
and proceed north to Jackson and
turn right. Continue two blocks to
LaSalle Street and turn left. Go
one block to corner of Adams and
LaSalle Streets.

Frank Lloyd Wright was no stranger to the design of Chicago's largest and most expensive office building of the late 1880s. The ten-story structure by Daniel H. Burnham and John Wellborn Root at the commercial center of the city housed the offices of Wright's clients, William Winslow and the Luxfer Prism Company. Wright himself maintained an office in the building from 1898 to 1899, although designing primarily from his suburban studio in Oak Park. Edward C. Waller, the building's manager and Wright's client as well, commissioned the architect to remodel the entrance and first-floor public areas of the Rookery.

Wright's design for the Adams and LaSalle Street lobbies included re-facing walls and encasing the intricate metalwork of courtyard columns with white marble, effectively unifying the three large, public, first-floor spaces. The incised and gilded relief of the marble panels reflects Wright's own interpretation of Root's ornamental schemes elsewhere in the building. Wright designed the suspended geometric light fixtures, replacing the large electroliers on the courtyard stairways with marble urns of similar scale.

Around 1930, a second remodeling was undertaken by William Drummond, a former Wright apprentice. Drummond's work is represented in the design of the entrance doors and the LaSalle Street elevator lobby. This National Historic Landmark in the heart of Chicago's financial district has undergone extensive restoration. An interpretive corner near the LaSalle Street entrance documents changes in the building's fabric through remodelings and restoration.

FRANK L. SMITH BANK

The simple dignity and solidity of the cut stone facade of this bank building, prominently situated on a small-town main street, is consistent with Frank Lloyd Wright's belief that banks should express their own character rather than "put on the airs of a temple of worship." Wright's view was surely influenced by his mentor Louis Sullivan, who first denounced the Roman temples that housed many banking enterprises. Independently, the two architects produced highly original solutions to the design of the Midwestern bank building.

Wright's early drawing of "A Village Bank," published in a 1901 issue of *Brickbuilder*, and later design of the Smith Bank, deliberately reject classical or historical references. A 1904 drawing documents an earlier design for the Smith Bank that shows a vertical, brick block with two columns flanking a recessed central entrance and a wide ornamental frieze on the upper level of the facade. Nothing is known of the architect's reason for abandoning this scheme.

The plan of the one-and-one-half-story, square building, as constructed, is as simple and forthright as its exterior presentation. A central entrance divided the public space into a banking room on one side, and a main office on the other. Space for three offices was reserved at the rear of the building. The walls are trimmed with narrow wood strips in a spare geometric pattern. Originally, a large skylight provided natural light and ventilation.

A 1991 remodeling and addition closely approximate the character and materials of the original structure. This project restored much of the bank's integrity diminished through earlier alterations.

1905

ADDRESS
First National Bank of Dwight
(currently)
122 W. Main Street
Dwight, Illinois
(815) 584-1212

MAILING ADDRESS
P. O. Box 10
Dwight, IL 60420

ACCESS
No organized tours.
Open business hours: Mon–Thurs
9 AM–3 PM, Fri 9 AM–6 PM.

DIRECTIONS
Exit I-55 on Route 17 or Route 47.
Continue into downtown Dwight.
Bank is on northwest side of railroad tracks that run diagonally through center of town.

GEORGE AND NELLE FABYAN VILLA

1907

ADDRESS
1511 Batavia Avenue
Geneva, Illinois 60134
(708) 741-9798

ACCESS
Museum hours: May–mid-Oct,
weekends and holidays 1–5 PM.
Weekday tours of ten or more,
by appointment only.
Donation welcome.

DIRECTIONS
From I-88 west of Chicago, take
Highway 31 north. Villa is just
south of Geneva.

Frank Lloyd Wright's typical Prairie-period work contrasts with his response to the constraints of this commission for the home of wealthy cotton-trader George Fabyan and his wife, Nelle, for what was then a 600-acre Fox River estate.

Incorporated into the north and west sections of the cruciform plan is an earlier L-shaped structure, which probably dictated the clapboard siding and gable roof. The shape of the roof is reflected in the second-story windows and the polygonal motif on the concrete piers. Wright added a two-story bedroom wing to the south, upper- and lower-level porches to the east, three verandas, and a courtyard screen fence. These ground-level, exterior structures visually balance the massive, heavily banded stucco eaves.

The 3,800-square-foot house contains four fireplaces of varied construction. The millwork is consistent with that found in Wright's Prairie houses. The pantry and first-floor bath are intact, along with a number of custom-made furnishings.

Both the villa and the large estate "Riverbank," with its Japanese garden and Dutch windmill, document the varied interests of the clients, which included the development of Riverbank Laboratories for research in cryptology, acoustics, physiology, and horticulture. The laboratory complex is located across the street and is not open to the public.

Since 1939, the estate has been owned and managed by the Kane County Forest Preserve District. In cooperation with the Friends of Fabyan, a volunteer group, the district has undertaken the preservation and restoration of the property.

RAVINE BLUFFS BRIDGE

1915

ADDRESS
Sylvan Road west of Franklin Road
Glencoe, Illinois

DIRECTIONS
From downtown Chicago, take
Edens Expressway (I-290) north
and exit at Dundee Road. Head
east and turn left on Glencoe
Road. Turn right on Maple Hill
Road and cross railroad tracks.
Turn left on Franklin and continue
to Sylvan. Turn left on Sylvan.

The Frank Lloyd Wright-designed bridge in this North Shore suburb of Chicago was constructed at the entrance to "Ravine Bluffs," a development commissioned by Sherman Booth, Wright's attorney. Only six of the planned residences—including Booth's own at 265 Sylvan Road—and the bridge were completed by 1921, when Booth's financial losses in the gold market brought an abrupt end to the speculative project. Wright had designed an elaborate estate for Booth in 1911, but the house, as built, is a much simplified version of the original plan. The bridge crosses the ravine and was intended to terminate in a porte cochere with a covered walkway leading to the house; these structures were never built.

The reinforced concrete deck of the three-span bridge is supported by three-foot-wide piers. The clear spans are twelve, fourteen, and twelve feet respectively. The center span has an inaccessible mezzanine located between the deck and floor of the ravine. The bridge accommodates a one-lane road and a pedestrian walkway with a semicircular seating area. Wright designed the low square urns and rectangular light pillars at each end.

Serious structural deterioration forced the closing of the bridge in 1977. Citizens campaigned to save the bridge from demolition, and in 1985 the bridge reopened after a $393,000 restoration.

EDWIN AND MAMAH BORTHWICK CHENEY HOUSE

1904

ADDRESS
520 N. East Avenue
Oak Park, Illinois 60302
(708) 524-2067

ACCESS
No tours.
Operated as a bed-and-breakfast
establishment; reservations
required.

DIRECTIONS
Take I-290 from Chicago to Oak
Park. Exit at Harlem Avenue and
head north to Chicago Avenue.
Turn right and continue to East
Avenue. Turn left on East Avenue
to house on right.

This typical Prairie-period dwelling is distinguished by its square plan and compact form. The main living area, which is above the level of the street, rests on a raised basement. A basement apartment was occupied by Mrs. Cheney's sister.

The house was originally enclosed completely by the high masonry wall and is exceptionally private. The secluded entrance is located on the side toward the rear of the house. The casement windows are grouped and raised above the gaze of passersby and the noise of the street.

The main living area stretches the full length of the front of the house. The massive masonry block of the fireplace, backed by a long gallery, bisects the interior with public spaces along the front of the house and bedrooms at the rear. The living room, at the center of the plan, opens to the dining room to the north and the library to the south. The wood trim of the walls and ceilings is of fir, stained dark red according to Wright's specifications.

In 1910 the board-and-batten garage was added, a year after Wright and Mrs. Cheney, who had been having an affair, took an extended trip together to Europe. In 1911, Cheney divorced his wife and remarried the following year; he remained in the house until the late 1920s. Mamah Cheney died tragically at Taliesin in 1914.

FRANCISCO TERRACE APARTMENTS ARCHWAY
RECONSTRUCTION

In 1895, Frank Lloyd Wright designed a two-story apartment building intended to house the working-class residents of what was then Chicago's Near West Side. The client, Edward C. Waller, was an important early patron of Wright's, whose many and large proposals included early social planning for the working poor.

The forty-four-unit building was designed around a large, central, rectangular courtyard. Although stair towers were located at the corners of the building block, each unit was also independently accessible from either the street or the courtyard.

After years of neglect, Francisco Terrace was demolished in 1974, despite attempts by local preservationists to save the structure. The archway, all cut stone, terra-cotta coping, and corner courtyard stair motifs were, however, dismantled and reconstructed in Oak Park at the entrance to a building of similar exterior design yet smaller scale and plan.

The large semicircular arch distinguishes the barrel-vaulted public entrance to the courtyard. The efflorescent terra-cotta ornament within the spandrels clearly reflects Wright's training with Louis Sullivan; the decorative effect is tightly framed by contrasting brickwork.

1895

ADDRESS
Euclid Place and Lake Street
Oak Park, Illinois 60302

DIRECTIONS
Take I-290 from Chicago to Oak Park. Exit at Harlem Avenue and turn right/north to Lake Street. Turn right on Lake and continue six blocks to Euclid Avenue. Archway is just past intersection on right.

HORSE SHOW FOUNTAIN
RECONSTRUCTION

1909

ADDRESS
Scoville Park Fountain
Lake Street and Oak Park Avenue
Oak Park, Illinois 60302

DIRECTIONS
Take I-290 to Oak Park. Exit at
Harlem Avenue and go north to
Lake Street. Turn right and
continue three blocks to Oak Park
Avenue.

Frank Lloyd Wright's role in the design of this fountain commissioned by the Horse Show Association is the subject of speculation. Richard Bock, the artist responsible for the sculptural ornament on a number of Wright-designed buildings of this period, is the designer of record. Bock credited Wright with suggesting the central opening to accommodate a drinking fountain; horses drank from square basins at the foot of the fountain. Historians generally agree that the naturalistic style of sculptural relief belongs to Bock. However, the overall geometric mass and proportions suggest a close collaboration between the sculptor and the architect.

The fountain, which today stands at the southeast boundary of Scoville Park, was reproduced in 1969 and sited 100 feet from its original curbside location.

UNITY TEMPLE

1905

ADDRESS
875 Lake Street
Oak Park, Illinois 60302
(708) 383-8873

ACCESS
Self-guided twenty-minute tours,
Mon–Fri 1–4 PM.
Adults $3, seniors and children
under age 18 $2.
Guided forty-five-minute tours,
Sat/Sun 1, 2 and 3 PM.
Adults $5, seniors and children
under age 18 $3.
Call for additional tours and
information.

DIRECTIONS
From Chicago, take I-290 to
Harlem Avenue. Exit and go north
to Lake Street. Turn right on Lake
Street. Unity Temple is one block
east of Forest Avenue at corner of
Lake Street and Kenilworth
Avenue.

When the Universalist Church of Oak Park was struck by lightning and burned in 1905, Frank Lloyd Wright was commissioned to design a new building for the congregation. He was faced with several major challenges: a congregation with modest financial resources insisting on a $45,000 budget when neighboring Gothic edifices typically cost in excess of $120,000; a small, long, and narrow site on a noisy and dusty main street; and the need for a building that provided separate spaces for worship and for socializing.

Wright's solutions, including the choice of reinforced concrete as the building material and the bold simplicity of the cubist design, were unprecedented. The material produced a monumental facade at minimal cost, afforded privacy, and muffled street noise. Ornament was cast into the form, eliminating the expense of a brick or plaster veneer. The flat, slab roof, also of concrete, cantilevers over the side walls to shelter the entrances and walkways.

Wright produced thirty-four studies before finalizing the design for the temple. He later remarked that it "looks easy enough now, for it is right enough." Indeed, the plan answered the congregation's need for functionally distinct areas: Wright had created two large spaces —a square sanctuary on the north and a rectangular meeting house on the south—connected by a shared central entrance hall.

Access to the building is through a raised terrace on either side. The low ceiling of the entrance hall contrasts dramatically with the two-story central space of the adjoining rooms. Low cloisters lead from the entry hall along the sides of the sanctuary to the rear of the room, so latecomers do not disturb a service in progress. Exits, however, are placed on either side of the pulpit, directing the congregants toward the minister as they depart. Tiers of seats enclose three sides of the room and accommodate 400 people, yet no congregant would be seated more than forty-five feet from the pulpit. This remarkably intimate space is enriched by the geometric patterns of the wood trim and the art-glass skylights typical of Wright's Prairie designs.

Unity Temple, the building Wright called "my little jewel box," was designated a National Historic Landmark in 1971. It has been in continuous use since 1908 by the congregation, now Unitarian-Universalist, that commissioned its design and construction. The building is one of seventeen structures designed by Wright to earn special recognition from the American Institute of Architects as representative of his contribution to American culture.

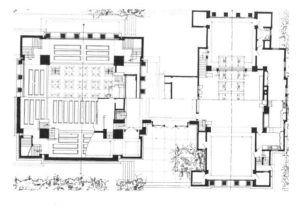

Frank Lloyd Wright was a twenty-two-year-old draftsman in the office of Chicago architect Louis Sullivan when he borrowed $5,000 from his employer to buy a corner lot and build a home for his bride, Catherine Tobin. The exterior of the house reflects an interest in the Shingle style designs then popular on the East Coast. The building also exhibits features that portend the mature Wright's philosophy of architecture: the emphasis on pure geometric forms, the broad, sheltering roof, the use of natural materials, and the unity of building and site.

Wright intended the living room fireplace hearth to be the center of family life. Thus, the plan of the first floor develops outward, pinwheeling from the masonry core of the living room and dining room fireplaces. The interior space is remarkably open, lacking the characteristic Victorian hierarchy of reception rooms, formal parlors, and related spaces reserved for public rather than family use.

In 1895, Wright expanded the living space of the home by adding a dining room and a barrel-vaulted playroom. The dining room was Wright's first attempt at totally unifying the design of a room, from integrated lighting and mechanical systems to furnishings and decorative arts. The barrel-vaulted playroom, with its massive fireplace, mural, skylight, built-in seating and cabinetry, offered a stimulating but practical space for the neighborhood kindergarten (directed by Wright's wife), and a recital space for a musically inclined family.

1889 / 1898

ADDRESS
951 Chicago Avenue
Oak Park, Illinois 60302
(708) 848-1976

ACCESS
Guided one-hour tours: Mon–Fri
11 AM, 1 PM, 3 PM; Sat/Sun
11 AM–4 PM, continuously.
Adults $6, seniors and children
under age 18 $4 (tours not recom-
mended for children under age 6).
Groups of ten or more by appoint-
ment only.
Other tours include a self-guided
walking tour of Frank Lloyd Wright
Prairie School Historic District and
"Wright Plus," a day-long tour of
ten buildings, third Saturday each
May ($45).
For group tour information and
reservations, call (708) 848-1978.

DIRECTIONS
From Chicago, take I-290 west to
Oak Park. Exit at Harlem Avenue.
Go north to Chicago Avenue. Turn
right and continue for four blocks.

LIMITED

In 1898, the young architect joined his professional and personal lives at one location with the addition of a four-room studio on Chicago Avenue. Comprised of a two-story, octagonal drafting room, reception hall, private office, and library, the studio was the birthplace of the first distinctly American style of design, the Prairie School. Wright employed fourteen apprentices and associates during his Oak Park tenure and completed the designs for at least 125 buildings, one-quarter of a long life's work.

The drafting room, a vertical space lit from above and encircled by a balcony, clearly sets forth the form Wright adopted for many great public commissions to follow: Unity Temple, the Larkin Administration Building (demolished), the Johnson Wax Administration Building, and the Guggenheim Museum. The home and studio served as a laboratory for Wright's ceaseless experimentation with light, space, and decorative forms.

In 1909, Wright left Oak Park, returning only briefly to remodel the building into two separate residences. Eventually the building was sold and further divided into apartments. In 1974, the Frank Lloyd Wright Home and Studio Foundation was established to acquire the building and restore it to its 1909 design. This National Historic Landmark is among seventeen buildings designed by Wright to earn special recognition from the American Institute of Architects as representative of his contribution to American culture. The building is one of twenty-four Wright-designed structures in Oak Park.

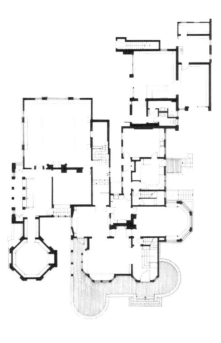

WALLER GATES

Six rock-face, cut-limestone pylons—set on concrete base skirts and topped with dressed-stone caps—and two metal fence sections remain from what was once the impressive entrance gate Frank Lloyd Wright designed for Edward C. Waller. A wealthy businessman and one of Wright's earliest patrons, Waller owned a six-acre estate along the Des Plaines River. In 1889, he commissioned the young architect to remodel the dining room of his twenty-four-room mansion and to design a gardener's cottage and stable.

The gates were constructed after Waller sold a portion of his land to William Winslow. In 1893 Wright designed a residence for Winslow that stands just inside the gateway at 515 Auvergne Place. The fence sections were almost certainly fabricated from rolled steel at William Winslow's ornamental ironworks. The original construction included a double drive gate over the roadway and two flanking walk gates. Square gaslight lanterns with brass frames topped the center piers.

The gates have been partially restored and the lanterns reproduced. The walkway and drive gates, which were similar in design to the fences, have yet to be reconstructed.

1901

ADDRESS
Auvergne Place at Lake Street
River Forest, Illinois 60305

DIRECTIONS
Take I-290 from Chicago to Oak Park. Exit at Harlem Avenue. Turn right and continue north to Lake Street. Turn left and continue for one mile, two blocks past light at Thatcher and Lake Streets.

SUSAN LAWRENCE DANA HOUSE

The thirty-five-room mansion Frank Lloyd Wright designed for Susan Lawrence Dana is the largest and most comprehensive example of the architect's Prairie-period houses to survive. Dana, a wealthy widow and social activist, wanted a house suited to her social ambition and lavish style of entertaining. The project, which began as a remodeling of the Lawrence family's 1868 home, soon eclipsed the earlier dwelling. Wright's double cross-axis plan incorporated vestiges of the original building in the foundation, walls, and fireplace in accordance with Dana's wishes.

Unfettered by financial considerations, the thirty-five-year-old architect faced both an unprecedented opportunity and formidable challenge. The project commanded the resources of his studio and several collaborating artisans for two years. The result was an extraordinarily complex and sophisticated integration of architecture, furnishings, and decorative arts, a complete and unified statement of the Prairie School aesthetic.

The massive, semicircular, arched entrance is an appropriately dramatic introduction to the 12,000-square-foot residence. The buff-colored brick of the exterior walls extends to an upper-level frieze of plaster panels, framing the art-glass casement windows. The gable roof and unusual flaring copper gutters lend an Asian character to the building.

1902—04

ADDRESS
Dana-Thomas House State Historic Site
301 E. Lawrence Avenue
Springfield, Illinois 62703
(217) 782-6776

ACCESS
Guided hour-long tours Wed–Sun
9 AM–4 PM.
Adults $3, students $1, children under age 3 free.
Groups of ten or more by appointment only (217) 782-6773.

DIRECTIONS
Take I-55 to South Grand exit. Go west on South Grand to 4th Street. Turn right (north) on 4th Street to Lawrence Avenue.

LIMITED

The principal public areas of the house—reception hall, dining room, and gallery—are centrally located on the raised first floor. These vast, open, double-height spaces with musicians' balconies were an ideal stage for concerts, lectures, and elaborate social gatherings. The lower level contained a billiard room, a bowling alley, and a library, among whose patrons were the neighborhood children.

Wright proved a brilliant manager of a project so large in scale. More than 450 pieces of art glass, including 200 light fixtures, and more than 100 pieces of oak furniture were designed and produced for the site. The exceptionally varied art-glass designs were inspired by butterflies and sumac plants. Richard Bock was responsible for the sculptures, and George M. Niedecken painted the dining room mural.

Dana remained in the house until 1928, and in 1944 the Thomas Publishing firm purchased the property. In 1981 the State of Illinois acquired the site. A $5-million restoration was completed in 1990.

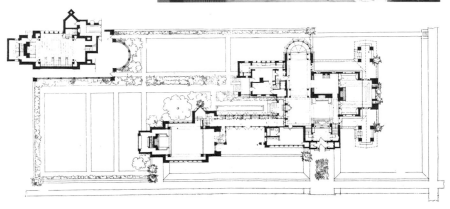

LAWRENCE MEMORIAL LIBRARY

1905

ADDRESS
Lawrence Mata Simpson
Resource Center
101 E. Laurel
Springfield, Illinois 62704
(217) 525-3144

ACCESS
No guided tours.
Library hours: Sept–May,
weekdays 9 AM–7 PM.
Summer by special appointment.

DIRECTIONS
Take I-55 to South Grand exit.
Head west on South Grand to
Second Street. Turn left on Second
to corner of Laurel.

Susan Lawrence Dana's patronage of Frank Lloyd Wright extended beyond the design of her magnificent residence at 301 E. Lawrence Avenue. She also commissioned the design of a small library as a memorial to her father, Rheuna Lawrence, president of the Springfield School Board at the time of his death in 1902. The library appears not to have opened until 1910, when Dana's contribution was recognized in the local newspaper. The commission was somewhat unusual as it required Wright to design an interior space within an existing building. The design is similar in plan to Dana's private library in her Springfield home.

The library was designed for the west room of a 1903 elementary school named in honor of Lawrence. During the 1930s, the room was dismantled to provide additional classroom space and was virtually forgotten. In 1982, the Dana-Thomas House was acquired by the State of Illinois; during the process of a historic building survey, Wright's drawings for the library were rediscovered, dispelling assumptions that the Lawrence Library was part of Dana's residence.

The library was reconstructed in 1992 and was furnished according to Wright's original design. A short, oak-spindled wall runs the length of the room, dividing the public reading area from the stacks. Four alcoves along the south wall are lined with bookshelves. The bookcases flanking the large east windows create recesses for window seats, and an L-shaped bench wraps the rear wall.

CITY NATIONAL BANK BUILDING
AND PARK INN HOTEL

Frank Lloyd Wright described the bank he designed for a business block in this turn-of-the-century prairie boom-town as a "strong box on a large scale, a well-aired and lighted fireproof vault."

The clients were lawyers in the firm Blythe, Markley, Rule and Smith. J.E.E. Markley was acquainted with Wright's work because his daughters attended Hillside Home School, a progressive boarding school near Spring Green, Wisconsin, run by two of Wright's aunts; Wright had designed buildings for the school in 1887 and 1902.

This large commission included the design of two buildings: the bank and an adjoining hotel. The bank's imposing facade dominated the corner lot; a sixteen-foot-high solid masonry wall formed the exterior of the ground floor. Brick piers with colored terra-cotta orna-ment extended from a sandstone beltcourse to the roofline, and framed the recessed art-glass windows. The top range of windows provided natural light for third-floor offices, while the smaller windows below formed the clerestory of the main banking room. Art-glass skylights, recently rediscovered, lit the one-story extension on the south side of the bank, which contained the president's office and the board room.

1909

ADDRESS
5 West State Street
Mason City, Iowa
(515) 424-1274

MAILING ADDRESS
McCoy and Company P.C.
P. O. Box 480
Mason City, IA 50401

ACCESS
No guided tours.
Building hours: Mon–Fri
9 AM–4 PM.

DIRECTIONS
From I-35, exit at Highway 18 and head east into Mason City to Highway 65. Travel north on 65 to State Street. Turn left on State and go one block. Bank is across from City Park.

The adjoining small-scale hotel faced the central park. The facility could accommodate fewer than fifty guests in the second- and third-floor bedrooms, but the first floor contained a full complement of guest facilities arranged around a front lobby. The dining room featured a large art-glass skylight, and the open porch on the second floor provided guests with a view of the park. Offices for the law firm were located on the second floor of the hotel's east wing, and on the top floor of the bank. They were entered by stairs from a first-floor entrance between the hotel and bank buildings. The hotel's west wing contained ground-floor retail space.

Construction was under way in 1909 when Wright left for a European sabbatical. In 1910, the space for the law firm was reconfigured to provide a larger library and additional offices; the building opened later that year. Construction costs for the bank were $65,000; for the adjoining hotel, $90,000.

The ground floor of the bank was converted to a retail space in 1926. Remodeling included the installation of large, street-level display windows, which compromised the impressive masonry exterior of Wright's design. In addition, a second floor of offices was located at the level of the former clerestory windows, which were enlarged, moving the horizontal beltcourse downward. Wright's design is faithfully represented by the upper-level ornamentation and wood-muntin windows.

The ground-floor hotel interior has been radically altered through numerous remodelings. The exterior has changed slowly with the loss of the ribbon windows on the third floor, the horizontal beltcourse beneath the balcony, and the large ornamental lanterns on the piers flanking the entrances, as well as from gradual deterioration with time.

GEORGE C. AND ELEANOR STOCKMAN HOUSE

Frank Lloyd Wright first published a variation on the plan of this compact Prairie style house as "a Fireproof House for $5,000" in a 1907 issue of the *Ladies' Home Journal*. Dr. G.C. Stockman was a friend of J.E.E. Markley and James Blythe, who commissioned Wright to design the City National Bank and Park Inn Hotel in Mason City.

The nearly square, first-floor plan of the Stockman House opens to a veranda on one side and a large entry hall with a cantilevered eave on the opposite side. The living room and dining room are essentially continuous, separated only by the fireplace block. The kitchen is at the rear, and the four bedrooms are all on the second floor. The house contains examples of Arts and Crafts and Wright-designed furnishings of the period.

The windows, in true Prairie fashion, are grouped in horizontal bands underscored by long window boxes. The projecting eaves extend the line of the low hipped roof, conveying a sense of shelter. The continuous wood trim wrapping the corners of the main block, as well as the dark window frames, roof fascia, and base, delineate the simple but subtle geometry of Wright's composition.

The house was the only Wright-designed residence actually built in Mason City, although the architect designed at least one proposal for a house in the Rock Crest subdivision. By 1917 this development contained eight dwellings designed by former associates and apprentices in Wright's Oak Park studio: Francis Barry

1908

ADDRESS
530 First Street, N.E.
Mason City, Iowa 50401
(515) 423-1923

ACCESS
June–Aug: Thurs–Sat 10 AM–5 PM,
Sun 1–5 PM.
Sept–Oct: Sat 10 AM–5 PM, Sun
1–5 PM.
Closed holidays.
Adults $3, children under age 11 $1.
May–Oct: guided tours for groups
of ten or more by appointment—
call (515) 424-3444.
Free guided walking tours of Rock
Glen/Rock Crest National Historic
District and slide lectures on Prairie
School Architects in Mason City
available for groups of ten or
more—call MacNider Art Museum
(515) 421-3666.

DIRECTIONS
From I-35, take U.S. 18 to Mason
City. In town, follow signs on U.S.
18 to State Street. Turn west at
"T" intersection and continue one
block. Turn right just over bridge.
Stockman House is located on
right and north of Rock Glen/Rock
Crest National Historic District.

LIMITED

Byrne, William Drummond, Walter Burley Griffin, and Marion Mahoney Griffin. Several of the houses share the open house plan, which, once published, was adopted by builders in many parts of the Midwest as an affordable, comfortable, family home.

In 1989 the Stockman House was moved to its present location, adjacent to the Rock Crest/Rock Glen National Historic District, where it is being restored by its current owner, the River City Society for Historic Preservation.

LOWELL AND AGNES WALTER HOUSE

ADDRESS
Cedar Rock
2611 Quasqueton Diag Boulevard
Quasqueton, Iowa
(319) 934-3572

A limestone bluff high above a bend in Iowa's Wapsipinicon River provided a stunning site for a complex of buildings that served as a summer retreat for Des Moines businessman Lowell Walter and his wife. The eleven-acre-site includes the main house, a two-story boathouse, an outdoor hearth, and an entrance gate. Walter commissioned the design in 1942, but wartime restrictions on materials delayed construction until 1948. In 1945, Frank Lloyd Wright published the design he referred to as a "glass house" in the *Ladies' Home Journal*.

The main living area of the Walter House is a 900-square-foot combined living room, dining alcove, and conservatory. Three exterior glass walls afford a spectacular view of the river and valley floor, while a central clerestory and skylights provide an interior garden with natural light. The plan extends from the main living area at an angle, in a wing containing the bedrooms, utility and storage areas, baths, and carport.

The walnut board-and-batten interior walls, cabinetry, and furnishings were all executed according to Wright's specifications. The bathrooms are Pullman-type modules installed as a unit. The heated floor mat is concrete, as is the roof with its broad overhangs and curved perimeter designed to support rooftop plantings.

According to provisions in Walter's will, upon his death in 1981, Cedar Rock became the property of the people of Iowa and is administered by the Iowa Department of Natural Resources.

MAILING ADDRESS
P. O. Box 1
Quasqueton, IA 52326

ACCESS
Free guided tours May–Oct:
Tues–Sun 11 AM–5 PM.
Groups of fifteen or more by
appointment.
Candlelight walk on second
Saturday each June.

DIRECTIONS
From I-80, take I-380 north to
Cedar Rapids. Continue on I-380
to Center Point exit. Go north on
Highway 920 through Center Point
seven miles to Walker. At big curve
in Walker, turn right on Linn
County Road (D62). Go to eastern
edge of Walker and turn onto
county road W35 to Quasqueton.
At northern edge of Quasqueton,
follow Cedar Rock sign north two
miles. Parking available at visitors
center.

HENRY J. AND ELSIE ALLEN HOUSE

Elsie N. Allen—wife of governor, senator and newspaper publisher Henry J. Allen—was responsible for commissioning Frank Lloyd Wright to design a home in College Hill, a newly developed residential neighborhood of east Wichita. By late 1915, Wright had designed the house, and by January of 1916, the Allens had received the plans. The house was roofed by late 1917, and the Allens lived there until 1949.

The Allen House is the last of Wright's Prairie period residences; it at once recalls the early Prairie houses and prefigures the Usonians of the 1930s. Wright designed the Allen House while working on designs for the Imperial Hotel in Tokyo; consequently, Japanese influences pervade the enclosed garden with its lily pool and garden house, reminiscent of a Japanese teahouse.

The plan of the residence is L-shaped. The entrance hall and 945-square-foot living room with a massive fireplace and bookshelf-lined alcove are contained in the one-story wing at the front of the lot. The two-story wing to the south comprises the first-floor dining room with an art-glass ceiling, kitchen, servant's quarters, and a two-car garage at ground level. On the second floor are Governor Allen's library, Mrs. Allen's study, bedrooms, and a guest suite.

The interiors are exceptionally rich, with art glass in windows and bookcase doors, as well as gold leaf

1915

ADDRESS
Allen-Lambe House Museum and Study Center
255 North Roosevelt Avenue
Wichita, Kansas 67208
(316) 687-1027

ACCESS
Guided tours by appointment only, $5 per person.

DIRECTIONS
From I-70, take I-135 and U.S. Highway 54 to Hillside and First Street. Take First Street (an eastbound, one-way street) to Roosevelt Avenue. Allen House is on corner of Roosevelt and Second.

LIMITED

applied to the horizontal joints of the masonry walls. The wood trim is sweet gum, and the window sashes are cypress. Walnut furniture designed by Wright in collaboration with George M. Niedecken, who built the furniture for a number of Prairie houses in the Midwest, is displayed throughout the house.

In 1990 the Allen-Lambe Foundation purchased the house and has undertaken its restoration.

JUVENILE CULTURAL STUDY CENTER

1958

ADDRESS
*Harry F. Corbin Education Center
(currently)
Wichita State University
Yale Avenue and 21st Street
Wichita, Kansas
(316) 689-3045*

MAILING ADDRESS
*Office of University Communications
and Relations
Wichita State University
Campus Box 62
Wichita, KS 67260-0062*

ACCESS
*No guided tours.
Center open when University in
session; Mon–Fri
9 AM–10 PM, Sat 9 AM–noon.*

DIRECTIONS
*From interstate, take I-135 to 21st
Street. Travel east on 21st Street
approximately 1.25 miles to
campus. Parking available in
lot south of center.*

LIMITED

Frank Lloyd Wright was commissioned in 1957 to design classroom, office, and laboratory space for Wichita State University's College of Education. Preliminary plans were completed in 1958, but inadequate funding delayed construction until 1963, when only one of two designed buildings was completed. The experimental elementary school was never built.

The concrete and steel structure is supported by 200 pylons sunk into a bed of unstable clay. An esplanade with a fountain and reflecting pool separates the center's two, 2-story wings, which contain class-rooms, offices, and support services. The interior floor is red vinyl tile. Trim, cabinetry, and custom furniture are made from solid, clear red oak. The exterior red brick was laid with matching mortar and raked horizontal joints. The fenestration includes large exposures of pol-ished plate glass, which were recently covered with bronze screen sunshades.

The natural-colored aluminum, arched traceries of the facade are repeated as design elements in other por-tions of the building. The roof fascia is exposed stone aggregate, colored to blend with the brick. The concrete canopies of the belvederes are rimmed with turquoise fascia. Slender light towers extend sixty feet through openings in the canopies.

JESSIE R. AND CHARLOTTE ZEIGLER HOUSE

Kentucky's only Frank Lloyd Wright-designed building stands within a few blocks of the state capitol. The Reverend Jessie Zeigler, a Presbyterian minister, may have visited Wright's studio and commissioned the design during a 1909 trip to Oak Park, Illinois, where he interviewed a prospective minister for the Frankfort area.

The design of the seven-room, 2,400-square-foot residence incorporates typical Prairie elements: open plan, broad eaves, horizontal wood trim, and bands of art-glass windows. The dining room sideboard was among Wright's favorite built-in furnishings, but the narrow oak cabinet suspended from the living room ceiling above the fireplace and wrapping back around the chimney block to the dining room is unique. Wright's drawings for the cabinets specified art glass in the door sashes, and interior electric lighting, which would create a lantern-like effect when lit at night.

Construction proceeded while Wright was in Europe. The distance of the site from the Oak Park studio and Wright's absence explain the quantity and detail of completed working drawings dated 1910. During a 1948 visit to the house, Wright evidently muttered that liberties had been taken with the design, probably referring to the suspended cabinet, which had been painted black and was being used as a bookcase.

The square plan with front and rear porches is a variation of the "Fireproof House for $5,000," published by Wright in the April 1907 issue of the *Ladies' Home*

1910

ADDRESS
509 Shelby Street
Frankfort, Kentucky 40601
(502) 227-7164

ACCESS
Guided tours by appointment only.
Adults $4, seniors and students $3.

DIRECTIONS
From I-64 follow signs to Kentucky State Capitol. Shelby Street is one block west of Capital Avenue.

Journal. The design of the art-glass windows and doors relies solely on simple geometric pattern, rather than color, for decorative effect. Each of the second-floor rooms offers direct access to a balcony, ensuring abundant light and cooling breezes during the hot summer months. Later alterations included the conversion of the second-floor rear balcony to a roofed sleeping porch, and the enclosure of the rear porch at ground level.

The house has been restored to its appearance in 1910–15.

GREGOR S. AND ELIZABETH B. AFFLECK HOUSE

The design of this 2,350-square-foot house demonstrates the adaptation of the Usonian plan to a steep site. Usonian was Frank Lloyd Wright's term for his moderately priced house for the average American, and the Affleck House is one of three such dwellings constructed between 1939 and 1941 in Michigan. Gregor Affleck had grown up in Spring Green, Wisconsin, and was acquainted with Wright's work and his mother's family. The residence cost $19,000.

The plan is T-shaped, with the entrance at the crossing. Access to the main living area is through a sky-lit loggia with an open well to a lower-level garden and stream. The functions of living, dining, and work rooms are consolidated in a unified space that spans a forty-foot ravine. A balcony wraps two sides of the cantilevered living room, and the bedroom wing anchors the house to the hill and terminates in a ground-level master suite.

The shiplapped cypress exterior walls replace the board-and-batten style of construction more typical of Wright's Usonian houses. The precision evident in the chamfered, overlapped boards and mitered corners attests to the skill of Harold Turner, a general contractor responsible for the construction of a number of the Usonians.

1940

ADDRESS
1925 N. Woodward Avenue
Bloomfield Hills, Michigan
(810) 204-2805

MAILING ADDRESS
Lawrence Technological University
c/o College of Architecture
21000 W. Ten Mile Road
Southfield, MI 48075-1058

ACCESS
Guided tours by appointment.
Donation requested.

DIRECTIONS
North of Long Lake Road on west
side of Woodward Avenue.

The Afflecks' children donated the house to the Lawrence Technological University in 1978. During the past decade, the University has undertaken the restoration of the building, which has included correcting structural problems, reconstructing deteriorated sections, improving energy efficiency, and restoring the original appearance of the house.

MEYER AND SOPHIE MAY HOUSE

Meyer May, a successful Grand Rapids clothier, and his wife Sophie commissioned Frank Lloyd Wright to design a family home in this western Michigan manufacturing town. The horizontal emphasis, concrete watertable, raked horizontal mortar joints, deep eaves, and rhythmic window groupings of their home are hallmarks of Wright's mature Prairie houses. Although more compact in scale, the lean masonry masses, concrete-capped walls, and projecting roofline of the May House recall Wright's design of the Robie House, under construction during the same year.

The May House is pushed back to the north lot line, providing maximum space for the garden and optimum exposure for the art-glass windows and doors of the south facade. The entrance is at the rear of the dwelling. Narrow stairs lead to the main living area where built-in cabinetry and screens fashioned of oak spindles in an open geometric pattern replace conventional walls as a means to define the interior space. The geometric oak trim throughout the house was scaled to the height of the owner, a fairly short man.

Wright specified the use of reflective gold glass in the mortar joints of the fireplaces, where its iridescent sparkle lightens the dense masonry wall. In form and

1908

ADDRESS
*450 Madison Avenue, Southeast
Grand Rapids, Michigan 49503
(616) 246-4821*

ACCESS
*Free guided tours Tues/Thurs 10
AM–2 PM, Sun 1–5 PM. Last tour
one hour before closing.
Reservations required for groups
of ten or more.*

DIRECTIONS
*Take U.S. 131 to Wealthy Street
exit. Travel east seven blocks to
Madison Avenue. Turn south and
continue for one block.
OR
Take I-196 to College Avenue exit.
Travel south on College to Logan
Street. Turn west on Logan to
Madison Avenue.*

LIMITED

color the art-glass design of the numerous windows, framed ceiling panels over recessed lights, and lanterns of the dining-room table draws its inspiration from abstracted plant forms.

George M. Niedecken, an interior designer and Wright collaborator, was responsible for the execution of the furnishings and decorative arts throughout the house, including the hollyhock mural dividing the gallery and dining room.

Completely restored by the Steelcase Corporation in 1987, the home offers a unique opportunity to experience the satisfying visual unity of an intact Prairie house.

LINDHOLM SERVICE STATION

Frank Lloyd Wright first began working on a design for a standard prefabricated gas station in the 1920s; the Lindholm Station is a variation of that prototype. The architect hoped to eliminate the frequent "eyesores" lining American highways, and to develop a facility that would offer a variety of customer services in addition to the sale of fuel.

When opened in 1958, the site attracted notice far beyond this small northern Minnesota town. Pump sales set a new record for Phillips 66. Unique features of the steel and concrete building include a sixty-foot illuminated roof-top pylon, an upper-level glass observation lounge, and a thirty-two-foot cantilevered copper canopy. Wright designed the canopy to hold overhead hoses, thus eliminating the obstruction of pump islands. The scheme was abandoned because local fire codes required underground fuel storage, but changes in regulation have inspired the owner to consider implementing Wright's original plan. Ceramic tile walls, cypress trim, decorative planters, and skylights in three of the four services bays were amenities that served to elevate the status of the humble filling station.

Although this building is the only Wright-designed service station ever built, the arrangement of service bays around a central office, the V-shaped canopy, and the large canted windows were elements incorporated into a number of Phillips Petroleum stations.

1956

ADDRESS
Best Oil Company (currently)
Route 33 and Cloquet Avenue
Cloquet, Minnesota 55720
(218) 879-0202

ACCESS
No organized tours.
Open regular business hours:
7 AM–6 PM daily.
Guided tours may be arranged in advance—call (218) 879-4666.

DIRECTIONS
From I-35, take Cloquet Highway 33. Go 4 miles and exit directly to site.

HERMAN T. FASBENDER MEDICAL CLINIC

Commissioned to house the general practice of Dr. Herman Fasbender, this building is one of four medical clinics that Frank Lloyd Wright designed between 1955 and 1957. Fasbender invited Tom Olson, a Taliesin apprentice and native of Hastings, to undertake the project. Olson deferred to Wright but participated in the building's design.

The entrance to the building faces State Highway 55, a major thoroughfare. The absence of windows and enveloping roofline effectively eliminated the distracting view and noise of the street, while promoting a sense of privacy for patients. The south side of the building, however, is almost entirely glass, providing ample light and a view of the extensive walled garden. A central hallway linked the reception area at one end of the building with five examination rooms, a private office, and a surgical suite. The tower visible from the front of the building housed X-ray equipment.

In the interest of economy, Fasbender chose to substitute sheet metal for the copper roof Wright had planned, but in 1994, new owners re-roofed the building according to Wright's original specifications. Fasbender occupied the building until 1967, when he joined another physician and built a larger facility. The building has housed a bank and a dental practice, and is now the office of a brokerage firm. While the space has served varied needs, the interior remains largely unchanged.

1957

ADDRESS
801 Pine Street
Hastings, Minnesota 55033
(612) 437-7440 or 437-1376

ACCESS
No organized tours.
Open regular office hours:
Mon–Fri 8:30 AM–5 PM.

DIRECTIONS
From I-494 take I-35 East and exit at Highway 52. Travel south, exiting at Highway 55, and head east to Hastings. Clinic is located at corner of Highway 55 and Pine.

COMMUNITY CHRISTIAN CHURCH

The building Frank Lloyd Wright planned for the congregation of Dr. Burris A. Jenkins was to be "the church of the future," but financial considerations, wartime shortages of materials, and restrictive building codes greatly compromised Wright's original design. Forced to abandon the planned parking terraces, rooftop garden, and rock ballast foundation, Wright lamented the building was his only in shape.

The angular facade and plan conform with the irregularities of the sloping site. Wright employed a rhombus with two, 120-degree angles and two, 60-degree angles as the basic unit in the design. Gunnite, an inexpensive, strong, fireproof, and lightweight concrete was sprayed over sheets of corrugated steel that were then sandwiched together to form the walls. The innovative material allowed Wright to reduce the thickness of the walls to a mere 2.75 inches. When joined at wide angles, the walls thus have the appearance of folded planes. The main stairwell and chancel are hexagonal.

A perforated dome was constructed on the roof of the chancel, but the searchlights necessary to illuminate Wright's envisioned "Steeple of Light" were not installed until 1994. Dale Eldred, an internationally known light sculptor, was commissioned to complete the lighting plan. On weekends and holidays, the lights—with a combined illumination of 1.2 billion candle power—project through the dome and reach several miles into the night sky.

1940

ADDRESS
4601 Main Street
Kansas City, Missouri 64112
(816) 561-6531

ACCESS
Free guided tours by appointment only: Mon–Fri 9 AM–4:30 PM. Self-guided tours regular business hours and Sun AM.

DIRECTIONS
Take I-70 to Broadway exit and head south on Broadway. Continue to 47th Street and turn left. Travel to Main Street and turn left. Go approximately one block to church on right.

Exceptional acoustics and seating for 900 people make the sanctuary a suitable space for musical performances as well as religious services. The small chapel, fellowship hall, and entrance from Main Street were later additions not of Wright's design.

LOCKRIDGE MEDICAL CLINIC

1958

ADDRESS
Brown and Blade Optometrists
(currently)
341 Central Avenue
Whitefish, Montana 59937

ACCESS
No organized tour program.
Building open regular business
hours, Mon–Fri 9 AM–5 PM,
Sat 9 AM–noon.

DIRECTIONS
Take Highway 93 into Whitefish.
Turn left on Third Street and go
one block. Turn right on Central
Avenue. Parking available in
office lot.

Frank Lloyd Wright's design of a one-story, brick and cast concrete medical clinic for the general practices of Drs. Lockridge, McIntyre, and Whalen has been significantly altered by subsequent owners. Shortly after the clinic was completed, Lockridge died; in 1964, the building was converted to a bank. In 1980, the bank moved to larger quarters, and the building was divided into three professional offices.

Wright's plan provided for a central waiting room and reception area with examination and procedure rooms to the side and rear. The floor-to-ceiling glass windows of the west facade and large fireplace with curved chimney breast and hearth have been retained despite considerable changes elsewhere. Wright's design also included a white plastic sphere that was centered between the windows at the front of the building. The sphere was half on the exterior and half on the interior, like the circular brick planter that supported it. The sphere was removed along with the interior section of the planter to provide space for a front walk and entrance to the former bank lobby.

The raked horizontal mortar joints and flush vertical joints reinforce the horizontality of the structure's exterior. The contrasting, light-colored, ornamental roof fascia is cast concrete, and the square planter on the roof now houses an air-conditioning unit. The carport to the south of the building is a later addition.

ISADORE J. AND LUCILLE ZIMMERMAN HOUSE

1950

ADDRESS
201 Myrtle Way
Manchester, New Hampshire 03104
(603) 626-4158.

ACCESS
Guided one-hour tours by
reservation only: Thurs/Fri 2 PM,
Sat/Sun 1 PM.
Adults $6, seniors, students, and
children $4. No children under 7.
In-depth, two-hour tour with musical entertainment and slide show:
Sat/Sun 2:30 PM.
Adults $10, seniors, students, and
children $7.
Group discount available for twelve
or more people.
All tours depart from Currier Gallery
of Art. June 1995–March 1996:
tours depart from satellite location
while gallery under construction.
Call (603) 626-4154 for tour
departure locations and directions.

DIRECTIONS
I-93 in Manchester to Exit 8
(Bridge Street). Follow Bridge
Street 1.5 miles to Ash and turn
right. Continue to Orange Street,
turn left to parking.

PLEASE
ARRANGE IN
ADVANCE

In their first letter to Frank Lloyd Wright, the Zimmer-mans described their "housing problem in ultra-conservative New England." Dissatisfied with the notion of building a traditional New Hampshire house, they wrote: "We wish to avoid adding a new antique to the city's architecture. It has been our dream to build a house that would be an integrated expression of our personal way of life rather than a coldly efficient building." Wright accepted the commission, designing what he called "a classic Usonian."

The brick, cast concrete, and cypress dwelling is sited diagonally on a one-acre lot. A high, continuous band of windows set in sand-colored concrete blocks relieves the solid masonry of the street facade. The garden facade, by contrast, is composed of floor-to-ceiling glass mitered at the corners.

Wright designed the landscape as well as all of the free-standing and built-in furniture; in addition, he even selected the textiles and the family's dinnerware. The use of built-ins, continuous concrete floor mat, and dramatic changes in ceiling height make this small house seem larger than its 1,458 square feet.

In 1952, the Zimmermans wrote to Wright telling him that theirs was "the most beautiful house in the world." The building was bequeathed to the Currier Gallery of Art in 1988 and has been restored by the museum.

GEORGE AND DELTA BARTON HOUSE

The Barton House is one of five residences Frank Lloyd Wright designed for employees of the Larkin Company between 1903 and 1908. Larkin Company executive and Wright client Darwin Martin introduced Frank Lloyd Wright to a small circle of Buffalo clients related either by family or employment.

The Barton plan borrowed directly from the 1902 design of the J.J. Walser House in Chicago. The contractor for the Walser House was the brother-in-law of another Larkin employee, William R. Heath, who may have recommended Wright's work to Martin initially. In September 1902, Martin and his brother William visited Wright's Oak Park studio, and both subsequently commissioned houses from him. In 1903, Wright began work on a house for Heath, which was not completed until 1905.

Darwin Martin commissioned the Barton House on behalf of his sister Delta and her husband George, also a Larkin employee. The dwelling was the first completed structure on the large corner site that would eventually include Martin's own house, which faced Jewett Parkway. The modest-sized house gave Wright an opportunity to prove himself worthy of the larger commissions Martin had in mind for the young architect, namely his own residence and the new headquarters of the Larkin Company.

The Barton House shares the cross-axial plan of the later and much larger Martin dwelling. The two-story main block contains the reception area, living

1903

ADDRESS
118 Summit Avenue
Buffalo, New York 14214
(716) 839-4496

ACCESS
Guided tours by appointment only.

DIRECTIONS
From I-90, take I-290 west; exit onto Route 33 West and then take Route 198 to Parkside Avenue. Turn right/north and continue to Jewett Parkway. Turn right, continue two blocks, and turn left on Summit Avenue.

room, and dining room on the first floor, with four bedrooms on the second floor. The first-floor rooms are joined in a continuous space with minimal separation. The significance Wright attached to the hearth as a symbol of family life is evident in the massive brick fireplace.

The single-story wing containing the covered porch and entryway, as well as the projecting kitchen on the opposite side, balance the vertical mass of the house. The rectilinear emphasis, low hipped roof, sheltering eaves, grouping of casement windows, broad chimney, and preference for materials used in their natural state are characteristics common to Wright's Prairie houses. The art-glass windows, doors, and light fixtures are all original; their chevron pattern is similar to that of the art glass designed for the Walser House.

Plan shows Barton (top right) and Martin (left) Houses.

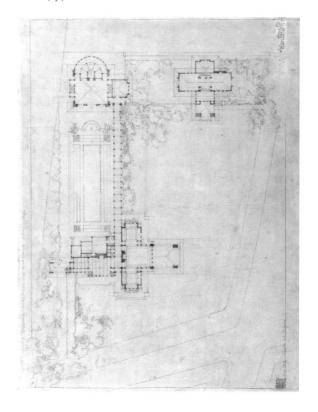

DARWIN D. AND ISABELLE R. MARTIN HOUSE

The Martin House, like the Dana House in Springfield, Illinois, was a grand and ambitious design to satisfy a wealthy client with strong personal convictions. Darwin Martin was the secretary of the Larkin Company, a soap manufacturing and mail-order company specializing in housewares. A successful, self-made businessman, Martin was an ideal client capable of financing and sustaining interest in a large and complex commission.

Through Martin's advocacy, Frank Lloyd Wright secured a number of commissions for residences for Larkin executives, but more significantly, he was selected to design the company's headquarters, the 1904 Larkin Administration Building (demolished in 1950).

Martin's private residence was part of a larger complex of six buildings Wright designed for the corner lot on Jewett Parkway. The greenhouse, conservatory, garage, and pergola were demolished in the 1950s to make room for several apartment buildings that now divide the former estate. A smaller residence for Martin's sister and her husband—the Barton House—faces Summit Avenue and is also open for tours.

Wright chose to square the house with the complex of buildings rather than with the parkway, as the lot lines were not parallel. The vertical dimension of the Roman brick building is compressed by the low hip roof

1904

ADDRESS
125 Jewett Parkway
Buffalo, New York 14214
(716) 839-4496

ACCESS
House temporarily closed for
restoration.

DIRECTIONS
From I-90, exit at Route 33 and
then take Route 198 to Parkside
Avenue (right/north); turn right on
Jewett Parkway, and go two blocks
to house.

and exceptionally broad eaves. Consistent with Wright's concern with relating a building to its surroundings, the pronounced horizontality of the dwelling reflects the prevailing flatness of the site.

The entrance hall bisects the cruciform plan of the house, connecting with a closed porch and extensive pergola that linked the main house with the conservatory. To the right, the library, living room, and dining room are aligned, their spatial continuity interrupted only by clusters of piers and partial walls. The freestanding brick piers contain the radiators used to heat the dwelling. The living room is relatively enclosed; its one exterior and windowed wall extends in a deep veranda. To the left of the entrance hall are the former reception room with an arched fireplace opening, an office, the kitchen, and the servants' dining room. The eight bedrooms of the house and a sewing room were located on the second floor. The basement contained an enormous billiard room and ballroom.

The coordinated effect of the art-glass windows, furnishings, light fixtures, and rugs, all of Wright's design, was spectacular. Orlando Giannini, a Chicago artisan who worked with Wright on a number of commissions, executed the gold mosaic wisteria mural. The Linden Glass Company, also of Chicago, was responsible for the copper-camed art glass in the casement windows. The wood trim throughout the house is fumed white oak. Mrs. Martin was an avid gardener, and Walter Burley Griffin of the Oak Park studio created the landscape design, including the semicircular perennial garden off the main veranda.

The Martin House is owned and operated jointly by the State University of New York, the State Office of Parks, Recreation, and Historic Preservation, and the Martin House Restoration Corporation.

SOLOMON R. GUGGENHEIM MUSEUM

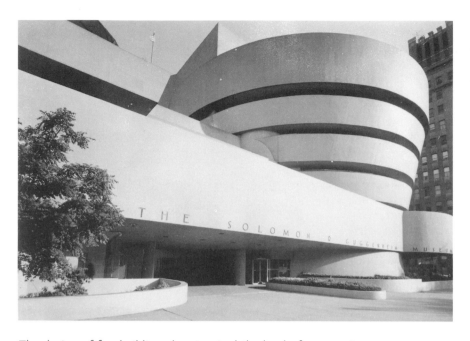

The design of few buildings has inspired the level of controversy generated by the Guggenheim Museum. Solomon R. Guggenheim commissioned the museum in 1943, but thirteen years passed before ground was broken. The design and construction of the museum required more than 700 drawings and an additional six sets of construction documents. Frank Lloyd Wright waged exhaustive battles with New York City officials whose outdated building codes had no relevance to his design. The museum opened shortly after Wright's death in 1959.

Wright's plan provided for several spaces: the main gallery; an adjoining, smaller circular structure, the Monitor Building, for administrative offices; and an annex, which was completed in a modified form in 1968 by Wright's associate William Wesley Peters.

Wright titled the gradually opening, cast-concrete form a ziggurat. The design is purely sculptural; there are no surface embellishments. The curving, stream-lined exterior establishes a pattern of wall and void that corresponds to changes in level on the interior. Inside the main gallery, a quarter-mile-long, cantilevered ramp curves continuously as it rises seventy-five feet to the roof. A twelve-sided, web-patterned, domed skylight

1956

ADDRESS
1071 Fifth Avenue (at 88th Street)
New York, New York 10128-0173
(212) 423-3500

ACCESS
Museum hours: Sun–Wed 10
AM–6 PM, Fri–Sat 10 AM–8 PM.
Adults $8, seniors and students $5.
Group discounts available for ten
or more people.
Closed Thursdays and Christmas
Day.
Architectural tours by appointment
only, including behind-the-scenes
breakfast tour guided by restora-
tion architects. Call (212) 423-3699
for information.

DIRECTIONS
By bus take M1, M2, M3, or M4 on
Madison or Fifth Avenues.
By subway, take 4, 5, or 6 on
Lexington Avenue line to 86th
Street. Walk northwest to museum.

covers the building and floods the interior with natural light. Works of art are displayed on the ground floor and in the seventy-four circular bays that line the walls of the ramp. A lower-level auditorium accommodates 300 people.

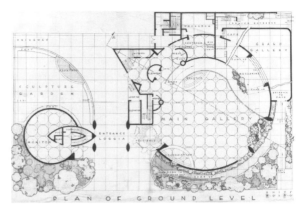

In 1989, construction began on a ten-story tower to provide an additional 31,000 square feet of exhibition space at the rear of the building. The expansion program also provided a 10,000-square-foot underground vault for administrative offices. In 1990, the museum closed for restoration, re-opening in 1992 with state-of-the-art climate control and security systems, new roofs, laminated, light-filtering glass in the skylights, a new cafe, and an expanded store. The Monitor Building was re-opened to the public as an exhibition space.

The Guggenheim Museum is one of seventeen structures designed by Wright to earn special recognition from the American Institute of Architects as representative of his contribution to American culture.

HOFFMAN AUTO SHOWROOM

Frank Lloyd Wright used glass and steel, materials he called basic tools of machine-age architecture, to complement the sleek, gleaming contours of the merchandise displayed in this Park Avenue showroom. The client, Maximilian Hoffman, was an early importer of European automobiles for the U.S. luxury car market. The curvilinear surfaces and mirrors visually expand this 3,600-square-foot, ground-floor space, which can accommodate five automobiles.

Mercedes-Benz Manhattan has occupied the showroom since 1957. In 1981, they hired Taliesin Architects, a division of the Frank Lloyd Wright Foundation, to supervise a restoration that included installing a previously unexecuted, mirrored Mercedes-Benz insignia in the showroom ceiling.

Hoffman also commissioned the design of a private residence overlooking Long Island Sound in Rye, New York. The house was completed in 1955.

1954

ADDRESS
Mercedes-Benz Manhattan (currently)
430 Park Avenue (at 56th Street)
New York, New York 10022
(212) 629-1666

ACCESS
No organized tours.
Showroom hours: Mon–Fri 9 AM–5 PM, Sat 9 AM–4 PM.

DIRECTIONS
By bus, take uptown Madison Avenue line to 56th Street. Walk one block east to Park Avenue. By train, take E or F and exit at "53rd on Fifth" stop. Walk 1/2 block east to Park Avenue.

FRANCIS AND MARY LITTLE HOUSE II
LIVING ROOM RECONSTRUCTION

Frank Lloyd Wright's last great midwestern Prairie house stretched 250 feet along the wooded shore of Lake Minnetonka. When all attempts by the Little family to find a suitable buyer or alternate use for the house failed in the early 1970s, the house was slated for demolition. At this point, the Metropolitan Museum stepped in to save parts of the structure. The Little House library has been installed in the Allentown Art Museum in Pennsylvania. The fifty-five-foot-long pavilion containing the living room crowned a knoll and functioned as a great public space for musical recitals and for entertaining. The house had two entrances; one led to a vestibule opening into the living room, while a separate door farther down the terrace led to the family's quarters. A small interior opening connected the two main areas of the house.

Every architectural and decorative detail contributed to the subtle and sophisticated visual harmony of this impressive space. Twelve paired art-glass panels were centered along each of the side walls. The pattern of clear and opaque white glass created a kind of decorative border framing views of the lake and the surrounding woods. The art-glass design was repeated in the clerestory windows and in the five laylights that were illuminated at night by electric lamps.

1912

ADDRESS
*The Metropolitan Museum of Art
American Wing
Fifth Avenue at 82nd Street
New York, New York 10028
(212) 879-5500 ext. 3791*

ACCESS
*Museum hours: Tues–Thurs and Sun 9:30 AM–5:15 PM, Fri–Sat 9:30 AM–8:45 PM.
Groups of six or more by appointment only.
Contribution suggested: Adults $7, seniors and students $3.50.*

DIRECTIONS
By uptown bus, take M1, M2, M3, or M4 on Madison Avenue; by downtown bus, take M1, M2, M3, or M4 on Fifth Avenue. By train, take 4, 5, or 6 to 86th Street and Lexington Avenue. Walk southwest to museum.

Correspondence between the architect and client documents how Wright somewhat reluctantly made several changes in the design of the art glass, including abandoning a green and yellow color scheme. The simplicity and minimal color of the final design pleased Little, who wanted no impediment to the lake view nor to the amount of natural light entering the room. Narrow bands of white oak trimmed the wall surfaces, framed the window and laylight openings, and extended across the coved ceiling, which reached a height of 14.5 feet.

The reconstructed room's furnishings are original Wright designs, although some were for the Littles' first house, which he had designed in 1902. Among the earlier pieces are the print table, the plant stands, the armchairs, and the reading table. The other furnishings, including six standing lamps, a library table, end table, and light fixtures, were executed as a group for this later house.

MEYERS MEDICAL CLINIC

Ohio gained ten of the state's eleven Frank Lloyd Wright-designed buildings during the 1950s; all were houses with the exception of this professional office building for Dr. Kenneth Meyers, a general practitioner.

A central entrance divides the structure into two main areas. A forty-four-foot-long rectangular waiting room with a massive brick fireplace extends to the northeast. The floor-to-ceiling glass windows and doors are mitered at the corner and open onto a terrace. The southern exposure affords the benefit of ample sunlight in winter, while the broad eaves shade the interior in the summer.

A corridor leads from the waiting room to an octagonal pavilion, in which wedge-shaped examination rooms are clustered about a circular work station. The clinic's plan originally provided for nine examination rooms, a library, and an X-ray facility. The library has been converted for conference and administrative space, and the X-ray room is now a surgical suite.

In 1989, the present owners constructed the built-in seating and plywood tables that Wright had designed for the waiting area. The carpet was custom-made to match the red-pigmented concrete floor Wright had specified for the property, which can still be seen on the terrace.

1956

ADDRESS
5441 Far Hills Avenue
Dayton, Ohio 45429
(513) 435-0031

ACCESS
No organized tours.
Open weekdays: 9:30 AM–4 PM.
Closed Mon afternoons, Thurs mornings.

DIRECTIONS
From I-675, exit at Route 48 (Far Hills Avenue). Travel north; clinic is on left.

CHARLES AND MARGARET WELTZHEIMER HOUSE

In the 1930s, Frank Lloyd Wright developed the concept of the Usonian house as part of Broadacre City, a utopian plan based on urban decentralization. The Usonian house was an efficient, comfortable, and attractive dwelling that Wright intended to match the needs and limited budget of the modern middle-American family.

The Weltzheimers, a family of six with a construction budget of $15,000, were ideal candidates. However, the completed house cost in excess of $50,000 in 1950, due in part to the relatively large scale of the dwelling, numerous changes made during construction, and extensive use of masonry and decorative millwork.

1948

ADDRESS
Weltzheimer-Johnson House
127 Woodhaven Drive
Oberlin, Ohio 44074
(216) 775-8665

ACCESS
Guided tours first Sun/third Sat of each month, hourly 1–5 PM. Last tour 4 PM.
$5 per person. No children under age 8.
Purchase tickets in advance at Allen Memorial Art Museum, Mon–Fri 10 AM–5 PM, Sat/Sun 12:45–4 PM. (216) 775-8665. Groups by reservation only, call (216) 775-2517.

DIRECTIONS
Head west on Lorain Street from Allen Memorial Art Museum to Pyle Road. Turn left and go three blocks to Morgan Street; turn left. Location is marked and driveway is located amid spruce trees between addresses 518 and 542. Parking allowed only on south side of Morgan Street.

The siting of the house, well back and at a forty-five-degree angle on a long narrow lot, affords maximum use and view of the property. The single-story, flat roof, and L-shaped plan with combined living and dining areas set at a right angle to the bedroom wing, are all consistent with earlier Usonian designs.

Other typical Usonian features include the use of built-in furnishings, cabinetry, and lighting to enhance the sense of interior spaciousness and preserve a unified style throughout the house. The clerestory windows and essentially glass wall on the southern aspect of the house minimize the distinction between the interior and exterior. The hemispherical ornament of the fascia and curvilinear cutouts in the clerestory panels are unique to the design of this house.

Mrs. Weltzheimer lived in the house until her death in 1963. Two subsequent owners made significant alterations, but in 1968 Ellen H. Johnson, an art history professor, purchased the house and undertook its restoration. She lived there until her death in 1992. The site is now owned and administered by Oberlin College.

PRICE TOWER

1952

ADDRESS
Northeast Sixth Street
at Dewey Avenue
Bartlesville, Oklahoma 74003
(918) 661-7471

ACCESS
Guided forty-five-minute tours,
Thurs 1:15, 1:45, and 2:15 PM.
Special tours and groups of twelve
or more by appointment only; con-
tact the Landmark Preservation
Council at Box 941, Bartlesville,
OK 74005
Donation suggested: Adults $3,
children $1.50.

DIRECTIONS
From Highway 75 in Bartlesville
take 60 West (Adams Boulevard)
toward Pawhuska. Turn right on
Dewey and proceed one block to
tower.

LIMITED

When Harold C. Price approached Frank Lloyd Wright
with the prospect of designing a building for his
Bartlesville pipeline construction firm, he envisioned a
two- or three-story structure with parking for ten trucks.
Wright immediately rejected the concept as inefficient.
Several months later, he presented Price with drawings
for a nineteen-story, 37,000-square-foot, multi-use
tower that would serve as corporate headquarters for
the company with additional space for apartments and
professional offices. Construction began in late 1953
and was completed in 1956.

The structural precedent for this "tower in a country town" was an unexecuted 1925 design for a New
York City apartment building, St. Mark's Tower. Wright
described the design as a tree-like mast; its concrete
floor slabs cantilever like branches from four interior
vertical supports of steel-reinforced concrete. Freed of
their load-bearing function, the exterior walls became
ornamental screens. The angled faces of the tower were
constructed from twenty-inch copper louvers that shade
the window surfaces, sheets of stamped copper, and
gold-tinted glass.

The 186-foot-tall building comprises a two-story base and a seventeen-story tower. Most of the upper floors contain four diamond-shaped units allocated for use as apartments or offices. The southwest quadrant has a separate entrance and elevator to serve eight, two-story offices. The nineteenth floor, not a full quadrant, was reserved for Price's office and a rooftop garden overlooking the city. Wright designed the built-in desk and glass mural, as well as a mural on the seventeenth floor.

In 1981, Phillips Petroleum purchased the building. The Price Tower is one of seventeen structures designed by Wright to earn special recognition from the American Institute of Architects as representative of his contribution to American culture.

The client and architect enjoyed an easy and mutually respectful relationship; Wright designed two houses for members of the Price family, one in Bartlesville in 1953 and one in Arizona in 1954.

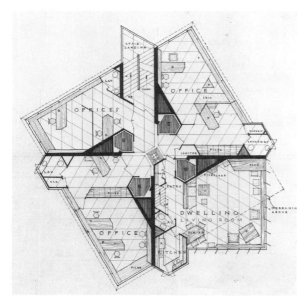

FRANCIS AND MARY LITTLE HOUSE II
LIBRARY RECONSTRUCTION

1912

ADDRESS
Allentown Art Museum
Fifth and Court Streets
P. O. Box 388
Allentown, Pennsylvania 18105
(610) 432-4333

ACCESS
General museum hours: Tues–Sat
11 AM–5 PM, Sun noon–5 PM.
Adults $3.50, seniors $3, students
$2, children age 12 and under free.
Free Sunday, noon–1 PM.
Guided tours for groups of ten or
more by appointment with four
weeks notice.

DIRECTIONS
Take I-78 to Exit 18A, Lehigh Street
north, and continue for one mile.
Bear left on Jefferson/15th Street.
Turn right on Turner and right
onto 5th Street. Street parking and
public lot nearby.

The extraordinarily large and complex home Frank Lloyd Wright designed for Francis and Mary Little in Wayzata, Minnesota, was among the richest expressions of the Prairie aesthetic. Before the building was demolished in 1972, critical sections were saved, including this library.

Originally located to the left of the house's asymmetrical entrance, the library functioned primarily as a reception area. Large art-glass windows on the east and south walls overlooked a terrace and the lawn respectively. The west wall was lined with oak bookshelves.

When the library was reconstructed, the architects followed a scheme used elsewhere in the house, and added concealed lighting and the parallel bands of oak trim to the ceiling. The furnishings are not original, but are consistent with Wright's style of interior design; the barrel chairs are reproductions of those he designed for several other homes, and the Wright-designed wall sconces in the Littles' living room were reproduced for this installation.

The library is one of two intact spaces from the Littles' Minnesota property on exhibit. The reconstructed living room is on exhibit in the American Wing of The Metropolitan Museum of Art in New York.

BETH SHOLOM SYNAGOGUE

1954

ADDRESS
8231 Old York Road
Elkins Park, Pennsylvania 19117
(215) 887-1342

ACCESS
Free guided tours by reservation:
Mon–Wed 10 AM–2:30 PM,
Sun 9 AM–1 PM (if no scheduled
activities).
Groups by appointment only.

DIRECTIONS
Take Pennsylvania Turnpike to
Willow Grove exit (Exit 27).
Travel south on Route 611 six miles
to Elkins Park.
OR
From Philadelphia, take I-95 north
to Cottman Street exit (Route 73).
Travel west to Route 611 (Old York
Road) and turn left. Go two blocks
to temple.

The complex symbolism embodied in the design of this synagogue for a Conservative Jewish congregation is the result of a close collaboration between Rabbi Mortimer J. Cohen and Frank Lloyd Wright. Every element of the design was carefully formulated to reflect some aspect of Jewish faith, history, or religious practice in a building whose character was distinctly contemporary.

The structure's hexagonal plan, according to Wright, mirrors the shape of cupped hands, as if the congregants were "resting in the very hands of God." Ramps leading from the entrance to the main sanctuary are intended to suggest the ascent of Mount Sinai. The pyramidal, translucent roof takes the form of the mountain, and the light filtering through its walls symbolizes the gift of the law. The projecting metal spines on the building's exterior represent the seven flames of the Menorah (the Jewish candelabra).

The 100-foot-high roof is supported by a frame of three 117-foot-long steel beams. The roof's faces are formed from a sandwich of wired glass on the exterior, and corrugated plastic on the interior. The main sanctuary can accommodate 1,100 people in seating arranged in triangular sections around two sides of the projecting pulpit. The forty-foot-high concrete monolith, representing the stone tablets given to Moses, forms a dramatic backdrop for the wooden ark containing ten Torah scrolls, one for each of the commandments. The aluminum and glass sculpture over the ark is entitled

"Wings." The colors of the triangular light fixture suspended over the pulpit symbolize divine emanations.

The building, completed in 1956, also contains a smaller, lower-level sanctuary that accommodates 250 worshippers, lounges, offices, and meeting rooms.

Haskell Culwell, the contractor for the Price Tower in Bartlesville, Oklahoma, was the contractor for the project. Beth Sholom Synagogue is one of seventeen structures designed by Wright to earn special recognition from the American Institute of Architects as representative of his contribution to American culture.

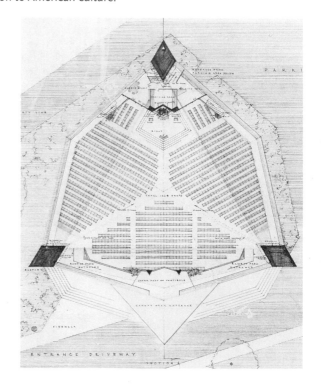

EDGAR J. AND LILIANE S. KAUFMANN HOUSE

1935

ADDRESS
Fallingwater
Route 381 South
Mill Run, Pennsylvania
(412) 329-8501

MAILING ADDRESS
P. O. Box R
Mill Run, PA 15464

ACCESS
Guided tours by reservation only:
April–mid-Nov, Tues–Sun 10 AM–4 PM.
Mid-Nov–March, Sat/Sun 10 AM–4 PM.
Adults $8 weekdays, $12 weekends;
family rates available.
In-depth tours:
April–mid-Nov, Tues–Sun 8:30 AM.
Mid-Nov–March, Sat/Sun 9 AM.
$30 weekdays, $35 weekends. Call
for weekday, student, senior, and
group rates. No weekend discounts.

Children under age 9 not allowed
to tour building, but may remain
at child care center on site.

DIRECTIONS
From I-76, take Exit 9. Continue
on Route 31 East for two miles.
Take Route 381 South for nineteen
miles. Fallingwater is on right.

LIMITED

The celebrated design of this country house for Pittsburgh department store magnate Edgar J. Kaufmann is the realization of Frank Lloyd Wright's romantic vision of man living in harmony with nature. Native rhododendron and mature trees cover the rugged slopes of the forested glen where a waterfall, fed by a mountain stream, inspired the design of this extraordinary dwelling. Wright told his clients that rather than simply look at the waterfall, he wanted them "to live with the waterfall...as an integral part of [their] lives."

Determined to build directly over the stream, Wright anchored a series of reinforced concrete "trays" to the masonry wall and natural rock forming the rear of the house. These terraces cantilever over the falls and seem to float above the valley floor. The man-made ledges extend the natural outcroppings and blend harmoniously with the rock formations of the stream bed below.

Rugged sandstone quarried on the site, concrete, and glass form the exterior and interior fabric of the building. The first-floor entry, living room, and dining room are integrated in a single continuous space. Rather than attempt to move an exceptionally large boulder, Wright simply incorporated it into his design, where it serves as the hearth. A hatch opening to a suspended stairway allowed for ventilation and access to the stream below. The upper floors are divided into bedroom suites opening onto private terraces. The wood trim through-out is black walnut, and the furnishings are intact. Walls of glass and wrap-around corner windows dissolve the boundary between interior and exterior spaces, opening the rooms to the surrounding tree tops.

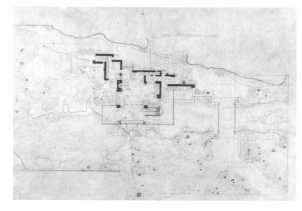

In 1938, Wright de-signed guest quarters set into the hillside directly above the main house. A covered serpentine walk-way links the two structures. In 1963, the Kaufmann family donated the entire property to the Western Pennsylvania Conservancy. Fallingwater is one of seven-teen structures designed by Wright to earn special recognition from the American Institute of Architects as representative of his contribution to American culture.

F.L. WRIGHT'S SAN FRANCISCO FIELD OFFICE
RECONSTRUCTION

1951

ADDRESS
Heinz Architectural Center
The Carnegie Museum of Art
4400 Forbes Avenue
Pittsburgh, Pennsylvania 15213
(412) 622-3289

ACCESS
Exterior viewing of office during
regular museum hours: Tues–Sat
10 AM–5 PM, Sun 1–5 PM. Closed
holidays.
Adults $5, seniors $4, students and
children under age 18 $3.

DIRECTIONS
Call (412) 622-3131.

Frank Lloyd Wright was at work on a number of California projects, including a design for a proposed bridge over San Francisco Bay, when former Taliesin fellow Aaron Green mentioned his plans to open a San Francisco office. Wright proposed a collaborative arrangement in which they would share an office, and Green would serve as field supervisor for Wright's California projects while developing his own practice.

The second floor of a four-story building at 319 Grant Avenue afforded a 900-square-foot space for the venture, and together, the two architects worked out the design. Rather than divide the limited area into small cells, the architects chose to delineate the space with two angled six-foot-ten-inch-high partitions. Constructed of plywood slats and translucent glass panes, the partitions afforded privacy and defined work areas without blocking the light from the streetside windows. The space accommodated a reception area, a drafting room, a conference room, a kitchenette, and a bath.

The materials used were inexpensive and readily available: the vinyl tile floor was in Wright's preferred shade of Cherokee red; the wood trim, cabinetry, and built-in furnishings were redwood plywood.

Wright used the office until his death in 1959. Green expanded his quarters to include the third and fourth floors of the building before dismantling and selling the second-floor office to the National Center for the Study of Frank Lloyd Wright. The office was acquired by the Carnegie Museum in 1992.

KALITA HUMPHREYS THEATER

Dallas is the home of the only commissioned theater ever completed from Frank Lloyd Wright's designs. As early as 1915, he was at work on "an experimental theater" for Aline Barnsdall, featuring a cycloramic, elevator stage and minimal separation between the actors and audience. In 1931 he designed the "New Theater" for Woodstock, New York, and in 1949, a similar structure for Hartford, Connecticut; none were executed.

The "New Theater," Wright believed, should free the stage of its traditional proscenium frame, and join the actors and audience in a unified space. In 1955, when approached by the Dallas Theater Center's building committee, Wright proposed adapting his earlier design for this urban site.

The reinforced concrete structure is built into the hillside of a one-acre, wooded site in the center of the city. Wright planned a zigzag approach from the parking lot to the entrance, providing patrons with ample opportunity to view the building's irregular massing.

The structure consists of a 127-ton cylindrical drum containing a forty-foot circular thrust stage with a revolving thirty-two-foot center platform. The drum, with its eight-inch-thick wall, is of cantilevered construction supported and anchored by the building's three-floor backstage area. The performing space can be extended through the use of the fixed apron, side

1955

ADDRESS
Dallas Theater Center
3636 Turtle Creek Boulevard
Dallas, Texas 75219
(214) 526-8210

ACCESS
Free tours by appointment only.
Mon–Fri 9 AM–5 PM (when
rehearsal not in progress).

DIRECTIONS
From Central Expressway, travel
west on Haskell, which changes to
Blackburn. Continue on Blackburn
for one block. Entrance is on left
just before Turtle Creek Blvd.

stages, and two balconies that flank the main stage. The house accommodates 466 people.

Other features of the building's design include dressing rooms on three levels and a spiral ramp leading to production workshops beneath the auditorium. Wright adamantly refused to allow the installation of a backstage elevator to facilitate the transfer of scenery. "I do not want my temple filled up with old, dirty scenery stage left and right," he pronounced. The elevator was installed without Wright's knowledge.

The theater was completed after Wright's death under the supervision of Taliesin Architects. Recent modifications include an upgrade to suspended stage lighting in the auditorium, and the addition of an office and rehearsal wing. The parking area and front lobby have been enlarged.

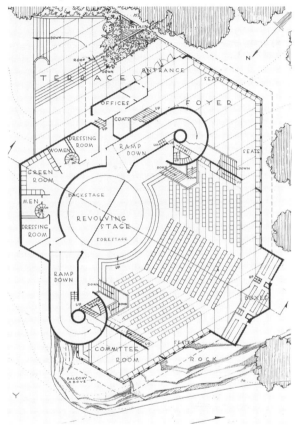

LOREN POPE HOUSE
RECONSTRUCTION

Frank Lloyd Wright designed this 1,200-square-foot house for Washington journalist Loren Pope and his wife at a total cost of $7,000. The radical nature of the design forced Pope to turn to his employer (*The Washington Evening Star*) for financing, and to hire a builder who refused to sign a contract.

As in most of the Usonian houses Wright designed as an economical solution to suit the needs of the average American family, the interior appears surprisingly spacious despite the modest scale of the building. The flat roof with a cantilevered carport, heated concrete floor slab, recessed lighting, and uniform treatment of the interior and exterior walls are features consistent with other Usonian designs. The house's decor is interpreted to the period of the early 1940s, and is complete with the plywood furniture that Pope and the builder constructed to Wright's specifications.

Destined for demolition by the state highway department, the house was donated by its second owner, Mrs. Robert Leighey, to the National Trust for Historic Preservation in 1963. The building was disassembled and moved fifteen miles from its original site in Falls Church, Virginia, to a similar wooded, hilltop site on the Woodlawn Plantation.

1940

ADDRESS
Pope-Leighey House
9000 Richmond Highway
Alexandria, Virginia
(703) 780-4000

MAILING ADDRESS
c/o Woodlawn Plantation
P. O. Box 37
Mount Vernon, VA 22121

ACCESS
Closed until March 1996 for restoration. Special construction tours may be given, call for information. Adults $5, seniors, students, and children (ages 6–12) $3.50. Group (minimum fifteen) discount available.

DIRECTIONS
From Washington Beltway (I-495), take Exit 1 south for Fort Belvoir. Approx. nine miles from beltway, follow signs for Woodlawn Plantation.

MONONA TERRACE

There is perhaps no greater acknowledgement of the enduring power of Frank Lloyd Wright's architecture than the decision of the city of Madison to build a $67-million convention center adapting a design Wright first developed fifty-six years earlier for the same site. Time has at last defeated the critics and detractors who continually frustrated Wright's attempts to secure a public commission in his boyhood hometown.

Wright's design of a large civic structure that would link the state capitol to the shoreline of Lake Monona is the anchor of an economic development program for downtown Madison. The plan began in 1938 as a city-county building with offices, courtrooms, a jail, and a railroad station. It went through a series of incarnations, re-emerging in 1941 and in the mid '50s as a civic and cultural center, and finally in 1960 as a municipal auditorium, exhibit hall, and community center. Despite Wright's willingness to modify the design to serve multiple purposes and interests, none of these projects garnered an adequate combination of public support and funding.

The interior has been reconfigured by Taliesin Architects in accordance with the building's new function, but the exterior of the structure and its profile and relationship to the site are consistent with Wright's 1959 design. The multi-story, steel and precast concrete, lakefront structure contains a 40,000-square-foot exhibition hall, a 15,000-square-foot ballroom and banquet hall, and a media center with seating for 320, as well as

1994
based on 1959 design

ADDRESS
One John Nolen Drive
Madison, Wisconsin
(608) 255-2537
(interim number for information)

MAILING ADDRESS
Greater Madison Convention and
Visitor Bureau
615 E. Washington Avenue
Madison, WI 53703

ACCESS
Scheduled to open in fall of 1997.

DIRECTIONS
Follow I-90 to U.S. Routes 12-18.
Exit west. Follow U.S. 12-18 to John
Nolen Drive and exit north.
Monona Terrace is visible crossing
Lake Monona Causeway.

meeting rooms and a 68,000-square-foot rooftop garden. The garden forms the terminus of a proposed
pedestrian mall extending from the capitol and nearby
government buildings. Pendentive arches frame expansive views of the lake from the interior exhibition lobby,
promenade, and community center. A curving lakeside
plaza, supported by concrete pylons driven into the lake
bottom, carries pedestrian and bicycle traffic and continues the linear shoreline park past the building. Spiral
ramps on either side of the building lead to parking
areas elevated over railroad tracks and a highway.

UNITARIAN MEETING HOUSE

1947

ADDRESS
900 University Bay Drive
Madison, Wisconsin 53705
(608) 233-9774

ACCESS
Guided tours mid-May–Sept,
Mon–Fri 10 AM–4 PM; Sat 9
AM–noon. Other times and
groups by appointment only.
Minimum donation $3.
Tour not recommended for
children under 12.
Building closes for two weeks
each August for maintenance.

DIRECTIONS
Exit I-90 at U.S. 12-18 and travel
ten miles to Verona Road (U.S. 18-
151 exit to Dodgeville). Exit north
onto Midvale Boulevard and continue to University Avenue. Turn
right and continue until second
traffic light (University Bay Drive);
turn left. Church entrance is at top
of hill on left.

Frank Lloyd Wright described the Unitarian Meeting House as a hilltop "country church," to be constructed of native stone and wood with a copper roof. Unitarian in character, he said, not simply an aggregation of steeple, meeting house, and parsonage, the mass of the building itself would give the impression of unity and aspiration.

Commissioned in 1946, the church took five years to build and cost three-and-one-half times Wright's initial estimate of $60,000. The willingness of members to devote countless weekends as construction volunteers helped contain costs. A herculean effort was required to haul more than 1,000 tons of limestone to the site from a quarry thirty miles away. Wright, too, felt personally invested in the project. His parents were among the earliest First Unitarian Society members, and he had officially joined the organization in 1938. He accepted a minimal fee, offered the assistance of Taliesin apprentices, and helped to raise funds by giving two lectures.

The design of the building is governed by a diamond module. The form is evident in the incised pattern in the concrete floor, the shape of the auditorium and hearth room, and the stone piers and planters.

The auditorium with its soaring ceiling and glass prow, in combination with the adjacent hearth room, can accommodate 340 people. A loggia leads to the west living room, where social functions are held. The auditorium and hearth room contain portable and collapsible benches and tables of Wright's design. The framing of the copper-clad roof, the building's most distinctive feature, set Wright at odds with local building commissioners who doubted its structural stability: the interior ceiling is actually much lower and does not conform with the angle of the exterior roof.

An education wing was added in 1964 and another hexagonal wing was added in 1990. Both were designed by Taliesin Architects. The copper roof over the hearth room and auditorium was replaced in 1994.

The Unitarian Meeting House is one of seventeen structures designed by Wright to earn special recognition from the American Institute of Architects as representative of his contribution to American culture.

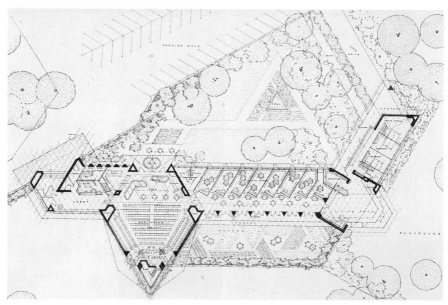

S.C. JOHNSON AND SON ADMINISTRATION BUILDING

Imagination, innovative technology, and client confidence combined to produce a revolutionary design for the corporate headquarters of the S.C. Johnson Wax Company. Herbert F. Johnson, grandson of the company's founder, was a successful businessman and a progressive manager. He envisioned a building that would provide a functional, pleasant working environment at the same time that it would project a modern corporate image. When completed in 1939, the building was hailed in *Life* magazine as the greatest innovation since the skyscraper: "a truer glimpse of the shape of things to come."

Since "nature was not present" in the bleak, surrounding, industrial landscape, the streamlined, curving brick face of the building is without conventional window openings. Frank Lloyd Wright "re-created nature" on the interior with a forest of slender, tapering "dendriform" columns that extend more than twenty feet from floor to ceiling, where they widen to support the eighteen-foot-wide concrete pads carrying the weight of the roof. The columns, constructed of high-strength concrete and steel mesh, taper to narrow bases, minimizing the loss of floor space.

The interior space was originally allocated according to the flow of work through the corporate organization.

1936

ADDRESS
S. C. Johnson Wax Company
Golden Rondelle Theater
1525 Howe Street
Racine, Wisconsin 53403
(414) 631-2154

ACCESS
Free, guided, half-hour tours by reservation only.
March–Nov: Tues–Fri 10 AM,
11:15 AM, 1 PM, 2:15 PM.
Dec–Feb: 11:15 AM, 1 PM only.
Tours do not include Research Tower.
Children under age 14 must be accompanied by an adult.

DIRECTIONS
From I-94, take Highway 20 exit and head east. After twelfth stop light (approximately eight miles) do not follow Highway 20 as it curves to left, but continue east onto 14th Street. Travel three blocks to Golden Rondelle Theater on right.

The company's clerical workforce occupies the 128-by-208-foot Great Workroom, middle managers the mezzanine, and executives the third-floor penthouse. Commonly used facilities and services are centrally located.

Wright's use of translucent glass tubing instead of transparent window glass was equally unprecedented. Originally, forty-three miles of layered Pyrex tubing formed the clerestories beneath the mezzanine and below the cornice line, as well as the sky-lit openings around the column capitals. Shadowless, natural light floods the interior, creating a workplace "as inspiring to live and work in as any cathedral ever was to worship in."

The building also contains a theater, circular stairs, and elevators. Wright designed the interior furnishings: three-legged chairs, and desks with swinging tills. Although extensively modified, the desks are still in use. A glazed, barrel-vaulted bridge connects the penthouse with offices created over the former squash courts.

The brick used in both interior and exterior walls was custom-made in 200 shapes to produce the necessary curves and angles. The horizontal mortar joints were raked to preserve the streamlined, horizontal effect of the masonry walls. Unlike most corporate headquarters with a central main entrance on the street facade, Wright efficiently placed the entrance at the rear of the building, opposite the carport.

In 1943, Johnson returned to Wright to design new quarters for the company's research and development division. The resulting fourteen-story research tower is connected to the main building by a covered bridge. Reinforced concrete slabs cantilevered from the building's central core form the alternating square floors and circular balconies. A central shaft contains the stairway, elevator, and mechanical systems. A second- and third-story addition east of the tower was executed in 1961 based roughly on plans by Wright. In 1978, two sculptures of Native Americans were installed in the Research Tower courtyard; these black granite figures of Nakoma and Nakomis were designed by Wright for an unexecuted Madison, Wisconsin, development in 1924.

The Johnson Wax buildings are among seventeen structures designed by Wright to earn special recognition from the American Institute of Architects as representative of his contribution to American culture.

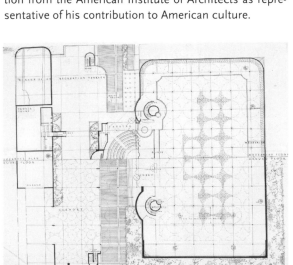

SETH PETERSON COTTAGE

1958

ADDRESS
E9982 Fern Dell Road
Reedsburg, Wisconsin 53959
(608) 254-6051 tours/general info
(608) 254-6551 rental reservations

MAILING ADDRESS
Seth Peterson Cottage Conservancy
Box 334
Lake Delton, WI 53940

ACCESS
Guided tours second Sunday of
each month, 1–4 PM.
First Sunday in June free.
Adults $2, members and children
under age 12 free. Discount for
groups of twenty or more.
Other times and groups of eight or
more by reservation only.

DIRECTIONS
Take I-90/94 to Exit 92 (Highway
12). Turn left/south toward
Baraboo and travel 1/4 mile to
Fern Dell Rd. Turn right on Fern
Dell and continue one mile past
Mirror Lake State Park entrance.

This 880-square foot building occupies a secluded promontory in one of Wisconsin's most popular state parks. The site was originally owned by Seth Peterson, a young man who prevailed upon Frank Lloyd Wright to design a small cottage. Peterson's untimely death in 1960 left the house unfinished and unoccupied. The building was sold, completed, and privately owned until 1966, when it was purchased by the state for park expansion.

A central fireplace divides the main living and dining area from the small kitchen, which abuts the single bedroom and bath. The exterior and interior walls as well as the fireplace are locally quarried sandstone. The interior flagstone floors are radiant heated. The flagstone extends beneath the exterior wall to become the floor of the terrace. The glass windows to the south, east, and west open the interior to the surrounding wooded site and lake view. The furnishings were executed from Wright's designs.

Prolonged neglect reduced the building to near ruin, before an extensive rehabilitation project was undertaken in 1989. Completed in 1992, the restored cottage was reopened for tours and vacation rental. Reservations must be made well in advance.

A.D. GERMAN WAREHOUSE

1915

ADDRESS
300 S. Church Street
Richland Center, Wisconsin 53581
(608) 647-2808 or (800) 422-1318
Richland Center Chamber of
Commerce

ACCESS
Guided 90-minute tours by
reservation, late May–Nov.,
or by special arrangement.
Adults $5, children under age 12 $2.

DIRECTIONS
Take Highway 14 to Richland
Center, turn right on Haseltine
Street, go two blocks to Church
Street, and turn right.

LIMITED

Albert Dell German, a Richland Center wholesale commodities dealer, planned to expand his business and commissioned Frank Lloyd Wright to design a new warehouse. Wright conceived a four-story, fifty-by-eighty-foot structure that rises from a concrete base. Its red brick exterior is crowned by an intricate frieze of contrasting grey concrete, and fifty-four windows are incorporated in the geometric design.

The flat-slab, reinforced concrete structure is designed with a grid of massive, steel-reinforced concrete columns with flaring capitals that carry the weight of the floor and roof. The capitals of six columns were designed with decorative motifs similar to the exterior frieze. The insulating effect of the double brick wall construction created a cold storage environment without mechanical refrigeration. Elimination of interior walls allowed maximum freedom of interior space.

By 1919, estimated construction costs that began at $30,000 had reached $125,000. German was forced to halt work on the warehouse and eventually lost the building through bankruptcy proceedings. Subsequent owners leased the building for storage and small-scale manufacturing.

During the 1980s, renovation provided for a gift shop and small theater on the first level; the second floor is an exhibit space dedicated to a retrospective of Wright's work.

TALIESIN

1911
rebuilt 1914 and 1925

Riverview Terrace Restaurant
(Taliesin Visitors Center): 1953
Hillside School (Taliesin Fellowship
Complex): 1902, 1932, 1933, 1952
Andrew and Jane Porter Residence
(Tanyderi): 1907
Romeo and Juliet Windmill: 1896, 1938
Midway Barns: 1938; dairy and machine
shed: 1947

ADDRESS
Highway 23
Spring Green, Wisconsin
(608) 588-7900

MAILING ADDRESS
P. O. Box 399
Spring Green, WI 53588

ACCESS
All tours depart from FLW Visitors Center,
at intersection of Hwys 23 and County C.
Visitors Center open daily April 1–Dec 15.
Call ahead to confirm days, times, and
fees, and for information on group, special,
and off-season tours.

Hillside Studio and Theater Tour:
One-hour, guided tours of studio and living
quarters of Taliesin Fellowship, theater, and
gallery. Daily 9 AM–4 PM.

Taliesin Country Walk:
Two-mile, two-hour walk through gardens
and grounds, including exteriors of all
major buildings. Daily.

Taliesin House Tour 1:
Two-hour tour featuring living room,
garden room, study, studio, sitting room,
and courtyards.
Daily except Wednesday. Reservations
required. Children under age 12 discouraged.

Taliesin House Tour 2:
Four-hour tour combining Hillside and
Taliesin interiors on all-inclusive tour includ-
ing areas not available on any other tour.
Limited offerings, reservations required.
No children under age 12.

Taliesin Preservation Tour:
Two-hour, work-site tour of restoration
projects on Taliesin estate. Limited
offerings, reservations required.

DIRECTIONS
Frank Lloyd Wright Visitors Center located 3
miles south of Spring Green on Wisconsin
River at intersection of Hwys 23 and County C.

Frank Lloyd Wright spent the summers of his adolescence roaming the farmland owned by his mother's family in southern Wisconsin. This experience fostered a love of the land and appreciation for nature that would inspire his philosophy of organic architecture. In 1911, he returned to this familiar ground to build a new home and life. Following family custom he gave the site a Welsh name, "Taliesin," which means "shining brow" and refers to the crest of the hill. The house, Wright explained, was not on the hill, but rather "of the hill, belonging to it, so hill and house could live together each the happier for the other."

The garden walls, terraces, house, and chimneys were constructed of native yellow limestone hauled from a nearby quarry. The long, thin, horizontal layers of stone simulate the natural strata of nearby outcropping ledges. The sand-colored upper walls recede beneath deep eaves, and the lines of the roof, too, were designed to conform with the slope of surrounding hills.

The interior demonstrates Wright's masterful orchestration of contrasting light, form, texture, and color in a harmonious composition. Entry is through a courtyard and low, narrow passage leading to the dramatic, light-filled space of the living room. Parallel bands of cypress trim accentuate the striking changes in ceiling height. Wood trim also wraps the walls defining the interior space. The massive stone fireplace is one of more than twenty in the complex. Numerous windows provide expansive views of the countryside.

Partially destroyed by fire in 1914 and 1925, the house was rebuilt and enlarged each time. In 1938, Wright began spending the winters at Taliesin West in Scottsdale, Arizona, but the Wisconsin site remained his primary residence. A home, a self-sufficient working farm, a studio, and eventually a school of architecture, Taliesin evolved over nearly five decades of Wright's residency. Buildings to house these many functions are linked variously by courtyards, loggias, and interior passageways in a sprawling 37,000-square-foot complex.

On adjoining land, Wright began designing buildings for members of his family as early as 1887 with Hillside School, a progressive, coeducational boarding school administered by his aunts Nell and Jane Lloyd Jones. In 1902, the school was redesigned, and the new building of ashlar-cut sandstone and oak demonstrates Wright's interest in using materials native to the site. The plan provided for a gymnasium, a laboratory, a drawing studio, an assembly hall, and classrooms. In 1932, Wright remodeled the space to accommodate the Taliesin Fellowship, an architectural training program. Changes included the construction of a 5,000-square-foot drafting room. The gymnasium was converted into a theater, the classrooms into galleries, and a dormitory was added to house the apprentices who came to study architecture the first year of the fellowship. The building continues to be used by the architectural school and by Taliesin Architects, the professional firm associated with the Frank Lloyd Wright Foundation.

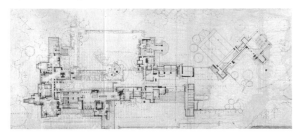

The Romeo and Juliet Windmill pumped water to Hillside School. The design of the sixty-foot-tower with interlocking octagonal and diamond-shaped forms inspired the Shakespearean reference. The board-and-batten exterior was originally shingled. The windmill is the oldest structure on the site and was restored in 1992.

In 1907, Tanyderi ("under the oaks") was designed for Wright's sister Jane and her husband, Andrew Porter. The exterior of the two-story, square, Prairie house is shingled, and the original, leaded, diamond-paned windows are intact.

Wright was equally concerned with the design of the lowly barn and toolshed, boasting that he could "build everything from a chicken coop to a cathedral." The long, low, red Midway Barns were constructed in the 1930s to house livestock; the dairy and machine shed were added the following decade. A geometric spire crowns the round, stone milkhouse. Architectural apprentices familiarized themselves with nature by sharing the responsibilities of managing the livestock, fields, and vegetable gardens.

In 1953, Wright designed the structure housing the visitors center as a restaurant to be frequented by guests at Taliesin. The octagonal, spire-topped pavilion, was intended as a drive-up facility for local farmers. The project languished until a resort developer purchased the plans and constructed the restaurant in 1967. Steel trusses from the flight deck of the Ranger, a World War II aircraft carrier training ship, were used to support the 300-foot-long structure. In 1993, the building was rehabilitated for use by the Taliesin Preservation Commission to serve as a visitors center.

Taliesin is a National Historic Landmark and one of seventeen sites designed by Wright to earn special recognition from the American Institute of Architects as representative of his contribution to American culture.

Opposite page (top to bottom):
Riverview Terrace Restaurant, Hillside School, Tanyderi, Midway Barns.
Above:
Romeo and Juliet Windmill.

ANNUNCIATION GREEK ORTHODOX CHURCH

Although Frank Lloyd Wright's design represents a distinct departure from traditional Byzantine church architecture, he retained the concept of a domed space and incorporated the symbols of the Greek Orthodox faith in his plan, which is essentially a Greek cross inscribed in a circle. Four equidistant, reinforced concrete piers support the structure and define the cross on the main floor. The lower-level space accommodates 240 congregants. Circular staircases lead to additional seating for 560 above. The sanctuary has no interior supports to obstruct the view of the parishioners, and no one sits more than sixty feet from the sacristy. The lower level of the church contains a circular banquet hall connected to an underground classroom wing.

Wright planned a dome 106 feet in diameter with a maximum height of forty-five feet that would completely encircle the structure. The dome's concrete shell is not fixed but floats on thousands of steel bearings contained in a circular channel beam that caps the outer wall. Originally covered with blue ceramic tile, the exterior of the dome is now covered with Neolon, a synthetic roofing

1956

ADDRESS
9400 West Congress
Wauwatosa, Wisconsin 53225
(414) 461-9400

ACCESS
Guided tours by appointment only
Tues/Thurs 9 AM–2:15 PM; fifteen
person minimum, no individual
viewing.
Appropriate attire required.
All ages $2.

DIRECTIONS
From I-94, take 894 bypass to 45
North toward Fond du Lac. Exit
Capitol Drive and travel east to
92nd Street. Head north to church.

material. Gold anodized aluminum is the principal metal used throughout the building. The symbol of a Greek cross inscribed in a circle was translated into a decorative element and appears throughout the sanctuary.

Light enters the church through semicircular windows and the 325 transparent glass spheres that crown the upper wall. Icons in the altar screen were by Wright's secretary, Eugene Masselink. The stained-glass designs in the lunette windows ringing the balcony are a recent addition, and are not of Wright's design. The building Wright called "a little St. Sophia" took two years to complete and cost $1.5 million to construct. The church was dedicated in 1961.

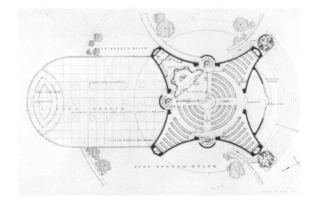

INTERNATIONAL SITES

GREAT BRITAIN
EDGAR J. KAUFMANN, SR., OFFICE
1937

ADDRESS
Victoria and Albert Museum, Cromwell Road, South Kensington
London SW7 2RL
0-1144-171-938-8500

ACCESS
Museum hours: Mon noon–5:50 PM, Tues–Sun 10 AM–5:50 PM.
Admission by donation.

DIRECTIONS
Nearest underground is South Kensington. Frank Lloyd Wright Gallery
located in museum's Henry Cole Wing.

JAPAN
IMPERIAL HOTEL ENTRANCE
LOBBY AND POOL RECONSTRUCTION
1915–22

ADDRESS
Museum at Meiji Mura, 1 Uchiyama, Inuyama-shi, Aichi-ken 484
011-81-568-67-0314
011-81-568-67-0358 fax

ACCESS
Hours: Mar–Oct 9:30 AM–5 PM, Nov–Feb 9:30 AM–4 PM.
Adults 1,500 yen, seniors and students 1,000 yen, children 600 yen.

DIRECTIONS
About 60 minutes from Nagoya. Non-stop bus from Meitetsu Bus Center,
or take Nagoya Railroad train or bus.

JIYU GAKUEN GIRLS' SCHOOL
1921

ADDRESS
2-31-3 Nishikebukuro, Toshima-ku, Tokyo, 171
03-3971-7535
03-3971-2570 fax

ACCESS
Guided tours by appointment only, Tues 10 AM–noon, 1–4 PM.

TAZAEMON YAMAMURA HOUSE
1918

ADDRESS
Yodoko-Geihinkan, 3–10 Yamate-machi, Asyiya-shi, Hyogo-ken 659
011-81-797-38-1720 tel and fax

ACCESS
House open 10 AM–4 PM. Ticket office closes at 3:30 PM.
Adults 500 yen, children 200 yen.
Temporarily closed due to damage sustained in 1995 Hanshin earthquake.
Call for information on re-opening.

ARCHIVES

ARIZONA
The Frank Lloyd Wright Archive
The Frank Lloyd Wright Foundation
Taliesin West
12621 N. Frank Lloyd Wright Boulevard
Scottsdale, Arizona 85261-4430
(602) 860-2700

CALIFORNIA
Getty Center for the History of Art and Humanities
401 Wilshire Boulevard, Suite 400
Santa Monica, California 90401
(213) 458-9811

Smithsonian Archives of American Art
Henry Huntington Library
1151 Oxford Road
San Marino, California 91108
(818) 405-7847

DISTRICT OF COLUMBIA
Manuscript Division, Library of Congress
Thomas Jefferson Building, Room 3004-5
Washington, D.C. 20540
(202) 707-5387

Prints and Photographs Division
Historical American Buildings Survey
Library of Congress
James Madison Building, Room 337
Washington, D.C. 20540
(202) 707-6399

ILLINOIS
Burnham Library, Art Institute of Chicago
Michigan Avenue at Adams Street
Chicago, Illinois 60603
(312) 443-3666

Oak Park Public Library
834 Lake Street
Oak Park, Illinois 60302
(708) 383-8200

Research Center
Frank Lloyd Wright Home and Studio Foundation
951 Chicago Avenue
Oak Park, Illinois 60302
(708) 848-1976

NEW YORK
Buffalo and Erie County Historical Society
25 Nottingham Court
Buffalo, New York 14216
(716) 873-9644

University Archives
State University of New York at Buffalo
420 Capen Hall
Buffalo, New York 14260
(716) 636-2916

Architecture and Design Study Center
Museum of Modern Art
11 West 53rd Street
New York, New York 10019
(212) 708-9547

Avery Architectural and Fine Arts Library
Columbia University
534 W. 114th Street
New York, New York 10027
(212) 854-3068

Department of American Decorative Art
The Metropolitan Museum of Art
Fifth Avenue at 82nd Street
New York, New York 10028
(212) 535-7110

WISCONSIN
State Historical Society of Wisconsin
816 State Street
Madison, Wisconsin 53703
(608) 262-3338

Prairie Archives
Milwaukee Art Museum
750 N. Lincoln Memorial Drive
Milwaukee, Wisconsin 53202
(414) 224-3200

WYOMING
American Heritage Center
University of Wyoming
Box 3924
University Station
Laramie, Wyoming 82071
(307) 766-6385

CANADA
Canadian Centre for Architecture
1440 Ouest, Rue Saint Catherine
Montreal, Quebec
Canada H3G 1R8
(514) 871-1418

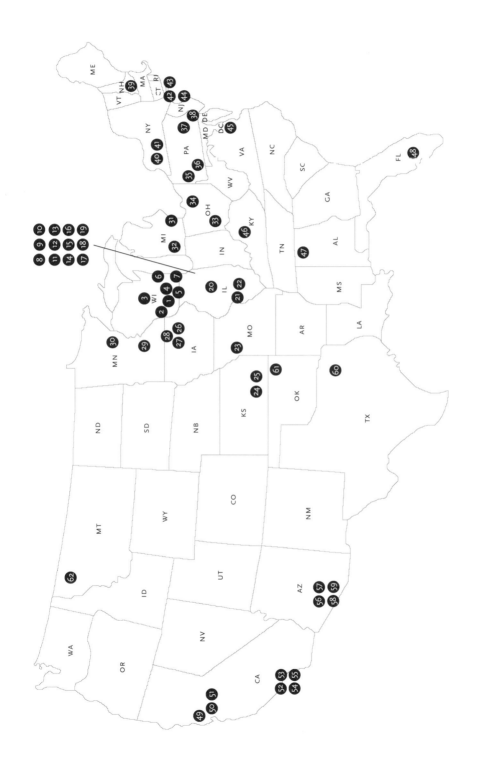

SUGGESTED ITINERARIES

For those interested in devoting several hours, a day, or a weekend to visiting publicly accessible Wright structures in a specific area, the following tours are suggested. Sites in the Chicago/Oak Park area and New York City are accessible via public transportation; all others require travel by car. Please check individual site listings for more specific information as well as seasonal closings. Call in advance to confirm building hours, tour schedules and options, fees, and directions to the site.

ARIZONA
PHOENIX DAY TOUR
Taliesin West, Scottsdale (several tour options)
Biltmore Hotel and Cottages, Phoenix
First Christian Church, Phoenix (weekdays)
Grady Gammage Memorial Auditorium, Tempe (weekdays, one hour from Taliesin or Phoenix)

Note: Taliesin tours start early in the morning. In the summer, plan to arrive as early as possible to avoid the heat. On weekdays take either the regular or behind-the-scenes tour at Taliesin. Continue on to the Arizona Biltmore Hotel for lunch. The hotel is about twenty-five minutes away by car.

As you leave Taliesin on Frank Lloyd Wright Boulevard, turn right on Shea Boulevard. Continue to Scottsdale Road and turn left. Continue to Lincoln and turn right. Follow signs for 24th Street Left. Continue on to Missouri and turn left to Biltmore.
Continue tour at First Christian Church. Leave Biltmore by turning left on 24th Street, continue to Camelback, and turn right. Go to Seventh Avenue (not Seventh Street) and turn right. Cross Bethany Home Road and Maryland to reach church, at 6750 North Seventh Avenue (corner of Ocotillo and Seventh).
To reach Gammage Auditorium (on Arizona State campus), exit church parking lot by turning left on Seventh Avenue. Turn right on Glendale Avenue and go to Squaw Peak Parkway, which leads to Highway 51. Go right (south) on Highway 51 to I-10. Exit at Broadway East and go two miles to Mill Avenue. Turn left and go north past 13th Street. Turn left at curve to continue on Mill Avenue. Turn right on Gammage Parkway to auditorium.

CALIFORNIA
LOS ANGELES SATURDAY AFTERNOON TOUR
Barnsdall House
Ennis House
Freeman House
Anderton Court Shops

Note: With the exception of the Anderton Court Shops, the Los Angeles sites are relatively close together. By coordinating a visit with the Saturday tours at the Ennis House, visitors with reservations could see the four Los Angeles sites in an afternoon.

Take Hollywood Freeway to Hollywood Boulevard exit. Start with one-hour noon tour of Aline Barnsdall House, 4808 Hollywood Boulevard.
Leave Barnsdall Art Park and turn right on Hollywood Boulevard. Continue to Vermont Avenue and turn left. Turn left on Glendower to Ennis House for 2 pm tour.

To reach Freeman House, return via Vermont Avenue to Franklin Avenue and turn right. Jog to left and turn right to remain on Franklin. Immediately on right is Methodist Church, where you can park before walking to tour site. On foot, turn right from church parking lot to Hillcrest. Go up Hillcrest to Glencoe and turn right. Continue walking about half a block down Glencoe to Freeman House, 1962 Glencoe Way.

Anderton Court Shops are about a thirty-minute drive away, and could be seen at end of day. Return via Hillcrest to Franklin. Turn right on Franklin and continue to Orange. Turn left on Orange and go to Sunset. Turn right on Sunset and proceed to Rodeo Drive. Turn left and continue about six blocks to 332 N. Rodeo Drive.

SAN FRANCISCO BAY AREA MORNING TOUR
Marin County Civic Center, San Rafael (weekdays)
V.C. Morris Gift Shop (Circle Gallery), Union Square
Hanna House, Stanford

Note: The Hanna House is approximately twenty miles south of San Francisco, but is temporarily closed for repair of earthquake-related damages. Write or call the Stanford Museum of Art for information on re-opening.

Take 10:30 am guided tour at Marin County and continue on to San Francisco via U.S. 101. Cross Golden Gate Bridge and continuing on Highway 101, proceed into center of city. Turn left on Post Street and go eight blocks to Union Square; Morris Gift Shop located at 140 Maiden Lane.

Hanna House is accessible from I-280. Take 280 south of San Francisco past Menlo Park to Sand Hill Road exit. Turn left to Stanford University campus.

ILLINOIS
All the Illinois sites could be seen in a three-day period, or selected Chicago and Oak Park sites could be combined in a two-day period, with visits to Wisconsin. Chicago is ninety minutes from Milwaukee, four hours from Madison, and five from Spring Green.

CHICAGO HALF-DAY TOUR
Charnley House
Rookery Building (weekdays)
Robie House

Note: The easiest way to visit these sites is to take a taxi. Information on public transportation (bus or train) is available by calling (312) 836-7000. Those who insist on driving will find navigating traffic a challenge and parking scarce and expensive. Start or end with noon tour of the Robie House in Hyde Park, south of the Loop.

Charnley House is north of Loop in residential neighborhood bordering southern section of Lincoln Park. Take Lake Shore drive north to North Avenue exit, which leads to Inner Drive. Turn left (south), following Inner Drive to Astor Street. Turn right to Charnley House, 1365 N. Astor Street.

To return to downtown area and Rookery Building, go south on Lake Shore Drive to Monroe and turn right. Turn right on Michigan Avenue, turn left on Madison, and left again on LaSalle. Rookery Building is at corner of LaSalle and Adams Streets.

To reach Robie House, about twenty minutes away on University of Chicago campus, take Adams Street east to Michigan Avenue and turn right. Turn left on Congress and right on Lake Shore Drive south. Exit at 53rd Street and go right to Woodlawn Avenue. Turn left to Robie House, 5757 S. Woodlawn Avenue.

One could also tour Robie House at noon and and then drive to Oak Park, about ten miles west of city, for one of several afternoon tour options.

OAK PARK AFTERNOON OR ALL-DAY TOUR

Frank Lloyd Wright Home and Studio
Unity Temple
Francisco Terrace Archway Reconstruction
Horse Show Fountain
Waller Gates, River Forest
Frank Lloyd Wright Prairie School of Architecture Historic District

Note: This suburb ten miles west of Chicago has twenty-four structures designed by Frank Lloyd Wright, two of which (the Frank Lloyd Wright Home and Studio and Unity Temple) are open to the public for tours. A recorded walking tour of the Frank Lloyd Wright Prairie School Historic District features the exteriors of several private homes. The recorded walking tour and building tours are offered as a two-and-a-half-hour package tour. Guidebooks and maps are available for those who wish to see all the structures in Oak Park and neighboring River Forest. Call the Frank Lloyd Wright Home and Studio Foundation (708) 848-1976 for information. During non-rush hour times, Oak Park is about a twenty-minute drive from downtown Chicago.

Go west on I-290 to Harlem Avenue exit. Go right (north) to Chicago Avenue and and turn right (east). Continue three blocks to Frank Lloyd Wright Home and Studio at 951 Chicago Avenue. Tickets, tour information, and maps are available at Ginkgo Tree Bookshop. Parking is available on street.

SPRINGFIELD AFTERNOON TOUR

Susan Lawrence Dana House (Wed Sun)
Lawrence Memorial Library (weekdays)

Note: Springfield is approximately three and a half hours south of Chicago. Weekday day trips from Chicago can include the Smith Bank in Dwight.

Take I-55 south and exit at Route 17. Go east two miles into town of Dwight; Smith Bank is on Main Street. Continue back on I-55 to Springfield and exit at South Grand. Go west on South Grand to Second Street and turn left. Continue to corner of Laurel. Lawrence Memorial Library located in Lawrence Mata Simpson Resource Center, 101 E. Laurel Street. To reach Susan Lawrence Dana House, go east on Laurel from First Street to Fourth Street. Turn left on Fourth and continue to Dana House on northwest corner of Fourth and Lawrence.

IOWA

MASON CITY AND QUASQUATON ALL-DAY TOUR

City National Bank Building and Park Inn Hotel (weekdays)
Stockman House
Walter House

Thursday or Friday, visit City National Bank in morning. Go east on State Street to Stockman House (fewer than five minutes). House located on right, just before bridge. Rock Crest/Rock Glen National Historic District immediately to left; Rock Glen enclosed by high stone wall. Parking available just north of Stockman House. Guided walking tours of Rock Crest/Rock Glen National Historic District available with advance reservations.

Walter House in Quasquaton approximately two hours' drive from Mason City. Take U.S. Highway 18 East to U.S. Highway 218 and go south. (Wright's Miller House, not open to public, in Charles City just east of Highway 218, one block south along Cedar River.) Continue on 218 through Waterloo to U.S. Highway 20 and go east. Take State Highway 282 south seven miles to Quasqueton and then go two miles west on 35E to Cedar Rock.

NEW YORK
NEW YORK CITY HALF-DAY TOUR
Hoffman Auto Showroom
Guggenheim Museum
Francis Little House Living Room Exhibit, The Metropolitan Museum of Art

Travel by bus or by train. Begin at Guggenheim Museum at Fifth Avenue and 88th Street, with breakfast or other architectural tours that can be arranged by appointment. Continue down Fifth Avenue by foot to Metropolitan Museum of Art at 82nd Street. Travel by bus (M1, M2, M3, or M4) to 56th Street. Walk one block east to Park Avenue; Hoffman Auto Showroom located at 430 Park Avenue.

WISCONSIN
Eight of forty-one structures designed by Frank Lloyd Wright in Wisconsin are open to the public, with guided tours. For a free tour guide send a self-addressed, stamped envelope to: Frank Lloyd Wright Wisconsin Heritage Tour Program, 3100 Lake Mendota Drive, #606, Madison, WI, 53705.

MADISON HALF-DAY TOUR (90 MIN. FROM MILWAUKEE)
Monona Terrace (to open in Fall 1997)
Unitarian Meeting House
Frank Lloyd Wright exhibits at the Elvehjem Museum of Art
State Historical Society of Wisconsin

Note: Monona Terrace and the State Historical Society (816 State Street) are located at the center of Madison's business district, near the State Capitol. The Elvehjem Museum is on the University of Wisconsin Campus and the Unitarian Meeting House is about twenty minutes away on the west side of the city.

From Monona Terrace, take John Nolen Drive/Blair Street and go three blocks to East Washington Avenue/ Highway 151; turn left. Go three blocks to Butler Street and turn right. Go three blocks to Gorham/University Avenue and turn left. Continue through downtown area to University Campus. Elvehjem Museum, with exhibits on Wright, located at 800 University Avenue. Continue on University Avenue and follow Campus Drive to University Bay Drive and turn right. Unitarian Meeting House is at 900 University Bay Drive.

MILWAUKEE AREA HALF-DAY TOUR (WEEKDAYS)
Annunciation Greek Orthodox Church (Tues/Thurs)
S.C. Johnson Administration Building (Tues-Fri)
Prairie School Archives at the Milwaukee Art Museum

Note: The Johnson Wax Building is thirty miles south of Milwaukee in Racine. A morning tour of the building could be followed by a tour of the Annunciation Greek Orthodox Church in Wauwatosa, a Milwaukee suburb, with an afternoon visit to the Prairie School archives at the Milwaukee Art Museum. Milwaukee is seventy-seven miles (ninety minutes) from Madison. A weekday morning tour of Johnson Wax would allow ample time to reach Madison and visit the Unitarian Meeting House or Monona Terrace in the afternoon. Racine and Madison are connected by I-94.

From Chicago or Milwaukee, take I-94 to Highway 20 and go east. After twelfth stop light bear to left onto 14th Street. Go three blocks to Golden Rondelle Theater of Johnson Wax Company to begin tour. Continue on to Milwaukee following I-94 and 894 bypass to Highway 45 North. Exit at Capitol Drive and go east to 92nd Street. Turn left to reach church at corner of 92nd and West Congress.

Prairie Archives of Milwaukee Art Museum are about fifteen minutes away in downtown Milwaukee. Follow Capitol Drive west to Highway 45 South and onto I-94 East to downtown Milwaukee. Continue on I-794E to Lincoln Memorial Drive. Go north to museum on right; 795 N. Lincoln Memorial Drive.

SPRING GREEN AREA TOURS (45 MINUTES FROM MADISON)
Taliesin (several tour options ranging from one to four hours)
German Warehouse, Richland Center
Seth Peterson Cottage, Reedsburg (2nd Sun. of month)

Note: Taliesin is about a five-hour drive from Chicago via I-90 and Highway 14, or a three-hour drive from Milwaukee, via I-94 and Highway 14.

From Madison, take Highway 14 to Route 23 and go south to intersection of 23 and Route C, site of Frank Lloyd Wright Visitors Center.

Tours of Taliesin can be combined with visits to German Warehouse in Richland Center, (about thirty minutes away), to Peterson Cottage in Reedsburg, Wisconsin (one hour north), or Unitarian Meeting House in Madison (forty-five minutes away). With advance planning, an overnight stay can be arranged at Peterson Cottage, allowing sufficient time to visit Wright sites in Milwaukee, Madison, and Spring Green areas.

To reach Richland Center, take Route 23 and go north to Highway 14. Go west to Richland Center and turn right on Haseltine Street. Go two blocks and turn right to German Warehouse, 300 S. Church Street.

To visit Peterson Cottage Conservancy, take Route 23 north through Reedsburg, following signs for Mirror Lake State Park. Turn right on Shady Lane, left on Mirror Lake Road, and right on Fern Dell Road, to cottage at E9982 Fern Dell Road.

INDEX

SELECT BIBLIOGRAPHY

Abernathy, Ann, and Thorpe, John, *The Oak Park Home and Studio of Frank Lloyd Wright* (Oak Park, IL: Frank Lloyd Wright Home and Studio Foundation, 1988).

Brooks, H. Allen, *The Prairie School: Frank Lloyd Wright and His Midwest Contemporaries* (Toronto: University of Toronto Press, 1972).

Bruegmann, Robert. "The Rookery Renaissance: Preservation's Touchstone." *Inland Architect* (July/August 1992): 50–57.

Buffalo Architectural Guidebook Corporation, *Buffalo Architecture: A Guide* (Cambridge, MA: The MIT Press, 1981).

Connors, Joseph, *The Robie House of Frank Lloyd Wright* (Chicago: University of Chicago Press, 1984).

Futagawa, Yukio and Pfeiffer, Bruce Brooks, *Frank Lloyd Wright Monographs* vol. 1–12 (Tokyo: A.D.A. Edita, 1987–88).

Gebhard, David, *Romanza: The California Architecture of Frank Lloyd Wright* (San Francisco: Chronicle Books, 1988).

Green, Aaron G., *An Architecture for Democracy: The Marin County Civic Center* (San Francisco: Grendon Publishing, 1990).

Gurda, John, *New World Odyssey: Annunciation Greek Orthodox Church and Frank Lloyd Wright* (Milwaukee: The Milwaukee Hellenic Community, 1986).

Haight, Deborah S. and Blume, Peter F., *Frank Lloyd Wright: The Library from the Francis W. Little House* (Allentown, PA: Allentown Art Museum, 1978).

Hallmark, Donald P., *Frank Lloyd Wright's Dana-Thomas House* (Springfield, IL: Illinois Historic Preservation Agency, 1990).

Hanna, Paul R. and Jean S., *Frank Lloyd Wright's Hanna House* (Carbondale, IL: Southern Illinois University Press, 1987).

Heckscher, Morrison and Miller, Elizabeth G., *An Architect and His Client: Frank Lloyd Wright and Francis W. Little* (New York: Metropolitan Museum of Art, 1973).

Hitchcock, Henry-Russell, *In the Nature of Materials* (New York: Duell, Sloan, and Pearce, 1942. Reprint, New York: Da Capo, 1973).

Hoffman, Donald, *Frank Lloyd Wright's Fallingwater: The House and its History* (New York: Dover, 1978).

Hoffman, Donald, *Frank Lloyd Wright's Hollyhock House* (New York: Dover, 1992).

Kaufmann, Edgar and Raeburn, Ben, ed., *Frank Lloyd Wright: Writings and Buildings* (New York: New American Library, 1974).

Lind, Carla, *The Wright Style* (New York: Simon and Schuster, 1992).

Lipman, Jonathan, *Frank Lloyd Wright and the Johnson Wax Buildings* (New York: Rizzoli, 1986).

Manson, Grant Carpenter, *Frank Lloyd Wright to 1910: The First Golden Age* (New York: Van Nostrand Reinhold Company, 1958).

McCarter, Robert, ed., *Frank Lloyd Wright: A Primer on Architectural Principles* (New York: Princeton Architectural Press, 1991).

McCoy, Robert E. "Rock Crest/Rock Glen: Prairie Planning In Iowa." *Prairie School Review* 5 (1968): 5–34.

Pfeiffer, Bruce Brooks, ed., *Letters to Clients: Frank Lloyd Wright* (Fresno: California State University, 1986).

Pfeiffer, Bruce Brooks and Futagawa, Yukio, *Frank Lloyd Wright: Selected Houses* vol. 1–8 (Tokyo: A.D.A. Edita, 1991).

Quinan, Jack, *Frank Lloyd Wright's Larkin Building: Myth and Fact* (Cambridge, MA: The MIT Press, 1987).

Rosenbaum, Alvin, *Usonia: Frank Lloyd Wright's Design for America* (Washington, DC: The Preservation Press, 1993).

Scott, Margaret Helen, *Frank Lloyd Wright's Warehouse in Richland Center, Wisconsin* (Richland Center, WI: Richland County Publishers, 1984).

Sergeant, John, *Frank Lloyd Wright's Usonian Houses: The Case for Organic Architecture* (New York: Whitney Library of Design, 1975).

Smith, Kathryn, *Frank Lloyd Wright: Hollyhock House and Olive Hill* (New York: Rizzoli, 1992).

Sprague, Paul E., ed., *Frank Lloyd Wright and Madison: Eight Decades of Artistic and Social Interaction* (Madison, WI: Elvehjem Museum of Art, University of Wisconsin, 1990).

Storrer, William Allin, *The Frank Lloyd Wright Companion* (Chicago: The University of Chicago Press, 1993).

Sweeney, Robert L., *Wright In Hollywood: Visions of a New Architecture* (Cambridge, MA: The MIT Press, 1994).

Wilson, Richard Guy and Robinson, Sidney K., *The Prairie School In Iowa* (Ames, IA: The Iowa State University Press, 1977).

Wright, Frank Lloyd, *An Autobiography* (New York: Duell, Sloan, and Pearce, 1943).

———, *The Living City* (New York: Horizon Press, 1958).

———, *The Natural House* (New York: Horizon Press, 1954).

ILLUSTRATION CREDITS

Frank Lloyd Wright	courtesy FLW Home and Studio Foundation
Rosenbaum House	Roy Simmons (ext. and int.), FLW Foundation (plan)
Arizona Biltmore Hotel	courtesy Arizona Biltmore (ext.), Hayes Button (int.)
First Christian Church	Don Kalec
Taliesin West	Pedro E. Guerrero (ext. and int.), FLW Foundation (plan)
Grady Gammage Memorial Auditorium	Arizona State University
Anderton Court Shops	Scot Zimmerman
Barnsdall House	Virginia Kazor (ext.), Scot Zimmerman (int.), FLW Foundation (plan)
Ennis House	Julius Shulman (ext.), Scot Zimmerman (int.), FLW Foundation (plan)
Freeman House	Julius Shulman
V.C. Morris Gift Shop	Julius Shulman (ext.), Scot Zimmerman (int.)
Marin County Civic Center	Glenn Christiansen
Hanna House	Leo Holub (ext. and int.), FLW Foundation (plan)
Florida Southern University	courtesy Florida Southern University
Pettit Mortuary Chapel	Don Kalec
Charnley House	Scott McDonald, Hedrich-Blessing
Robie House	Richard Nickel/Aaron Siskind, courtesy Richard Nickel Committee (ext.), Hedrich-Blessing (int.), FLW Foundation (plan).
Rookery Building Entry Lobby	Merrick, Hedrich-Blessing (int.)
Smith Bank	Jodie Bourne, Dwight Star & Herald
Fabyan Villa	courtesy Friends of Fabyan
Ravine Bluffs Bridge	Don Kalec
Cheney House	Don Kalec
Francisco Terrace Archway	Don Kalec
Horse Show Fountain	Don Kalec
Unity Temple	Melissa Pinney (ext.), Jonathan Lipman, AIA (int.), FLW Foundation (plan)
FLW Home and Studio	Don Kalec (ext.), Jon Miller, Hedrich-Blessing (int.), FLW Home and Studio Foundation (plan)
Waller Gates	Don Kalec
Dana House	Doug Carr (ext. and int.), FLW Foundation (plan)
City National Bank/Park Inn Hotel	courtesy Lee P. Loomis Archive of Mason City History
Stockman House	Robert McCoy (ext.), Jonathan Lipman, AIA (int.)
Walter House	Don Kalec (ext.), Ezra Stoller, © Esto (int.)
Allen House	Wesley Ellington
Juvenile Cultural Study Center	Jim Meyer, Media Resources Center, Witchita State University
Zeigler House	Art Meripol, © Southern Living, Inc.
Affleck House	courtesy Lawrence Technological University (ext.), Wally Bizon, Lawrence Technological University (int.)
May House	courtesy Steelcase, Inc.
Fasbender Medical Clinic	courtesy Dave Karel, Garlock-French Roofing
Community Christian Church	Don Kalec (ext.), Bob Greenspan (int.)
Lockridge Medical Clinic	Scot Zimmerman
Zimmerman House	courtesy Currier Gallery of Art (ext.), Bill Finney, courtesy Currier Gallery of Art (int.)
Barton House	Jack Quinan
Martin House	Buffalo and Erie County Historical Society (ext.), University of Michigan, Ann Arbor (int.), FLW Foundation (plan)
Guggenheim Museum	Robert E. Mates (ext.), David Heald (int.), FLW Foundation (plan)
Hoffman Auto Showroom	courtesy Mercedes-Benz of North America
Little House Living Room	Cervin Robinson, The Metropolitan Museum of Art, Emily Chadbourne Bequest
Weltzheimer House	courtesy Oberlin College
Price Tower	courtesy Phillips Petroleum (ext. and int.), FLW Foundation (plan)
Little House Library	courtesy Allentown Art Museum, gift of Audrey and Bernard Berman, 1972
Beth Sholom Synagogue	Jonathan Lipman, AIA (int.), FLW Foundation (plan)
Kaufmann House	Robert P. Ruschak, courtesy Western Pennsylvania Conservancy (ext.), Kenneth Love, courtesy Western Pennsylvania Conservancy (int.), FLW Foundation (plan)
FLW's San Francisco Field Office	Joanne Devereaux, courtesy The Carnegie Museum of Art
Kalita Humphreys Theater	courtesy Dallas Theater Center (ext. and int.), FLW Foundation (plan)
Pope House	Roy Blunt, courtesy National Trust for Historic Preservation
Monona Terrace	Jim Anderson for Taliesin Architects
Unitarian Meeting House	Eugene Casselman (ext. and int.), FLW Foundation (plan)
S.C. Johnson and Son Admin. Bldg.	courtesy S.C. Johnson Wax (ext. and int.), FLW Foundation (plan)
Peterson Cottage	Clair Kilton
A.D. German Warehouse	Pedro E. Guerrero
Taliesin	Pedro E. Guerrero
Annunciation Greek Orthodox Church	Pedro E. Guerrero (ext.), Don Kalec (int.) FLW Foundation (plan)
Jiyu Gakuen Girls' School	Jonathan Lipman, AIA